À LA CART

A SUPPLIER'S GUIDE
TO RETAILERS' PRIORITIES

"A must read for anyone remotely involved in the retail grocery business.

I am applying your advice in my business plan, your wisdom has provided clarity and focus."

"Peter Chapman's book (à la cart) should be mandatory reading for anyone who really wants to thrive as a supplier in the food industry."

"In a fast changing retail landscape with the introduction of big box stores, mass merchandise and drug channels plus the effect of National procurement, Peter showed me how to develop meaningful relationships with customers that created real value for both our Dairy operation and the retailers."

"To date there has not been a playbook that outlines the do's and don'ts of doing business in the Canadian grocery industry; you have rectified the situation – well done."

"The Canadian food processing industry is facing enormous competition in domestic markets from suppliers located all over the globe. Peter's book provides invaluable insight for all Canadian processors on how to make their products and their company, the preferred supplier of choice to Canadian grocers. This is necessary reading for businesses of all sizes, whether they are new to the industry or experienced suppliers."

À LA CART

A SUPPLIER'S GUIDE
TO RETAILERS' PRIORITIES

PETER CHAPMAN

à la cart
A supplier's guide to retailers' priorities

© 2014, GPS Business Solutions
11 Condor Rd
Bedford, Nova Scotia, Canada B4A 3K9

ISBN 978-0-9936734-0-5

Published by GPS Business Solutions

For more information about the retail landscape or
getting your item in to the shopping cart contact :
   GPS Business Solutions
   (902) 489-2900
   or visit our website
   www.gpsbusiness.ca

Chapman, Peter
Printed in Canada

CONTENTS

INTRODUCTION. VII

PREFACE. IX

CHAPTER 1 1

SURVIVE AND THRIVE IN THE COMPLEX FOOD INDUSTRY

> The difference between customers and consumers
> Introduction to retailers' priorities
> Importance of priority alignment

CHAPTER 2 11

SALES ARE JOB #1 FOR RETAILERS

> Momentum is everything
> Sales culture
> Sales planning

CHAPTER 3 29

DIFFERENTIATE TO SURVIVE

> A crowded retail landscape
> The format is the brand
> Support differentiation

CHAPTER 4 53

SUPPLY CHAIN — THE UNSUNG HEROES

> Getting product to the shelf is expensive
> Retailers' focus on efficiencies
> Embrace procurement, warehousing and distribution

CHAPTER 5 67

FOOD SAFETY IS NON NEGOTIABLE

> Food safety keeps retailers up at night
> Audits and programs
> Responsibility of suppliers

CHAPTER 6 79

HEALTH & WELLNESS SELLS PRODUCTS

> Consumers are changing how they shop
> Retailers' investments in programs
> Sales opportunities

CHAPTER 7 95

GLOBAL FOODS ARE ON FIRE

The faces and tastes of our consumers are changing

Global foods drive traffic and sales

Become a more valued supplier

CHAPTER 8 107

FOOD SOLUTIONS ARE MORE POPULAR THAN EVER

Consumer demand for quick and easy

Retailers' efforts to retain food dollars

Sales and profit are available early

CHAPTER 9 121

CORPORATE SOCIAL RESPONSIBILITY
— DO THE RIGHT THING

Transparency with consumers

Retailer specific initiatives

Solidify the supplier-retailer relationship

CHAPTER 10 145

THRIVING IN THE FOOD INDUSTRY

Essential ingredients for priority alignment

Implementing priority alignment

Align, align, align

CONCLUSION 163

THE RECIPE FOR SUCCESS

THE LANGUAGE OF RETAILERS 164

RESOURCES 168

ACKNOWLEDGEMENTS 169

ABOUT THE AUTHOR 170

INTRODUCTION

Our retail landscape is constantly evolving and food is a powerful traffic builder. Traditional food retailers are competing with more diverse competition every year. This book is for suppliers and other people involved in the food industry to help them understand what is important to their customers. Everyone involved in the food industry needs to understand what retailers are doing and why they are doing it.

The chapters in the book are designed to share why a priority is important to the retailers, what they are doing about it and how suppliers need to address the priority in their own business. The final page of each chapter is an opportunity for the reader to include some specifics from their own business.

During the planning process it is easy to focus on your own business and the opportunities within. Every supplier or business involved in the food industry should be aware of the retailers' priorities when they conduct their business planning. The final chapter provides a process for this to ensure there is alignment, which leads to prosperous relationships.

PREFACE

There were so many times when I was sitting across the desk from a supplier when it was apparent an item would not achieve its full potential. Two thoughts would come to my mind:

You just don't understand me as a retailer;

It's your job to get the item in the shopping cart, not mine.

I know our respective sales would have been much greater if the discussion was built on these two key points. These discussions can be more productive and there are so many opportunities for suppliers who see the retailer as a customer. Despite a common goal, relationships between retailers and suppliers can be very adversarial, an oddity that happens when each party does not understand or respect the challenges facing the other.

One of my biggest frustrations was suppliers who believed their job was to produce a product and get it listed. Retailers have thousands of items to manage and sell, so here's a clue to your success; they will only keep the ones that make it through the cash register. Suppliers have to produce products and entice the consumer to make the decision to purchase.

During my twenty years with Canada's largest food retailer the retail landscape and the sales mix changed dramatically. Suppliers need to evolve with the changes. I saw items that should have performed so much better. It really was disappointing to see items perform poorly when they had so much potential. Collectively we can have such a powerful influence over what the consumer buys. I am committed to helping suppliers understand the retailers so that they will be more successful.

The chapters in this book are designed to help suppliers and others in the food industry understand what is important to the retailers, what the retailers are doing about it and how suppliers can incorporate this in to their own business. I will take you behind the closed doors of the retailers to offer some insight in to the most important issues and how the retailers are trying to drive traffic and sales.

Products will be successful when they are aligned with retailer's priorities and when they resonate with consumers. We all win when products get to the shelf and the consumer puts the item in the shopping cart.

Peter Chapman

CHAPTER 1

SURVIVE AND THRIVE IN THE COMPLEX FOOD INDUSTRY

WHY DO WE HAVE TO MAKE THIS SO DIFFICULT?

Selling food products should be such a simple business: you produce a product, deliver it to a store and watch the consumer put it in their shopping cart. Unfortunately, the industry has made it so much more complex. Today's food industry is a myriad of challenges, throughout the entire value chain. I will explain what the retailers are doing and why. There are suggestions for suppliers that will conclude with a recipe for success.

To be successful the supplier must satisfy two masters:
1. The customer who is the retailer;
2. The ultimate consumer.

CUSTOMERS AND CONSUMERS ARE NOT THE SAME

There is a fundamental difference that can be the determining factor between success and failure. In our system of food retail, the retailer issues the purchase order and is the customer of the supplier. The consumer rarely ever pays the producer for the product; they buy it from a retailer.

The *customer* pays a business for a good or service;

The *consumer* purchases a product for personal consumption.

I have seen many great products that do not succeed because the supplier has only focused on the consumer. It's critical to understand who your customer is and what they are focused on today and into the future.

There are great opportunities for suppliers who **commit to understanding 'the retailer is the customer.'** I believe that by understanding and anticipating the needs of retailers and consumers, suppliers can become much more valued and in demand.

PRODUCTIVE RELATIONSHIPS REQUIRE BOTH PARTIES TO UNDERSTAND AND RESPECT EACH OTHER. ENSURE YOUR ORGANIZATION UNDERSTANDS AND RESPECTS THE PRIORITIES OF THE RETAILER.

There are thousands of great food products being produced today and in development for production tomorrow. It continues to amaze me how people can introduce new items and reinvent old ones. Just when you think you've seen them all, a new item will hit the store shelves that generates a loyal following of consumers. It is vitally important to understand that retailers control the store shelf. Category managers decide if it will be available before the consumer ever has a chance to put it in their shopping cart.

A well defined customer base is very important. In food processing, there are many options for selling product. Make sure you explore all avenues to find the right fit for your business. It is important to remember that medium and large retailers are not going to change their methods of operation for suppliers — you need to understand them and design a business model that will be successful satisfying their needs.

Selling product to the retail trade can be challenging, however, there are some benefits that are often overlooked.

The challenges include:

1. Large retailers can exert influence over suppliers;
2. Selling product to large retailers can be intimidating to smaller suppliers;
3. A small number of category managers can have a significant influence over the success or failure of a producer or processor;
4. The retailer has made the investment in the store so they control what goes in;
5. Product specifications and standards are often challenging for producers and processors to meet;
6. Central distribution is difficult for some producers and processors to accept;
7. Central procurement often requires travel and developing relationships with people in different regions;
8. Retailers have their own language and they expect suppliers to understand the terms and words they use *(see page 164: The language of retailers)*.

There are also many benefits to selling product to the medium and large retailers:

1. A small number of customers allows the producer or processor to really understand the customer in detail;
2. Retailers focus on volume which can be a benefit to suppliers;
3. Improvements in the retailers' distribution systems can result in cost savings for producers and processors;
4. The focus of retailers is relatively consistent. The overall priorities are similar. They each have their own version of sales as a priority but all have sales as a top priority;
5. The expectations of retailers are well defined;
6. The resources within retailers are becoming more limited, therefore, when you provide a valuable service to them you have increased your value.

YOU HAVE TO KNOW WHAT YOUR CUSTOMER IS DOING!

If you determine retailers are the best distribution channel for your products, you must understand the priorities of your customers. These are key areas of focus for the retailers, where they are investing money and resources to be successful. The business priorities among different retailers are surprisingly, relatively consistent.

SALES

Sales are a top priority of every retailer. To be successful they have to get their products through the cash register. This is the first number they look at each week. It is critical that your products will deliver sales to the retailers every week. You should have targets for sales within your business and if possible relate them to your own metrics as well as to the retailers. For example: you might require 10,000 cases per month to get the level of efficiency required for your packaging equipment, but you should also quantify that in terms of cases per week per store. That's how your customer measures success. Look at sales within your business and through the eyes of your customer.

DIFFERENTIATION

In a crowded marketplace, **every retailer is trying to carve out its own niche.** It is critical for suppliers to treat each retailer with a unique strategy. Every retailer is trying to sell food but each has its own method of doing it. Suppliers must understand this and develop a solution that supports the point of differentiation for each retail banner.

SUPPLY CHAIN

Getting the product through the supply chain to the store is very costly and complicated. **All retailers are working to improve efficiency** and reduce the costs of the tasks involved. This is one area of the retailer's operation that is not only expensive, aside from getting product to the store, but delivers very little value to the consumer. The end users expect the product will be there for them in pristine condition, but there is no premium for getting product to the shelf in great condition. Therefore, retailers are very focused on moving products as efficiently as possible. It is critical to the success of an item and a supplier that products flow through the entire supply chain system properly. This starts when the purchase order is issued and ends when the product gets to the store shelf.

FOOD SAFETY

The topic of **food safety has become a non-negotiable issue** in the supply of food to retailers in our marketplace. Retailers have their standards and expectations for food safety and it is the responsibility of suppliers to understand these and meet or exceed them. Suppliers who do not have adequate processes in place run the risk of providing unsafe food and seriously impacting the relationship with retailers.

HEALTH & WELLNESS

As consumers learn more about the impact of food to their bodies, shifts have occurred. People are looking to move back to products which are better for them. **People want to live longer and healthier.** Food producers and retailers are changing the products and stores to accommodate these changes in the marketplace.

GLOBAL FOODS

Our population is changing and consumers are becoming exposed to more and more diverse tastes and products. The growth of sales in the ethnic categories is driven by immigration and access to information. The world is a much smaller place in terms of ingredient sourcing and cooking methods. First, second and third generation Canadians are looking for many products that were never available in Canada, even 10 years ago. Food producers and retailers are responding quickly to make these items available. There are many opportunities for suppliers who are able to produce these products or bring these items into the country.

FOOD SOLUTIONS

One of the most valuable commodities to the consumer is time. **Producers and processors who are able to reduce preparation time and effort will generate sales.** The new caveat to this opportunity is that items should also provide some health benefit. The end user is focused on reading nutrition labels and finding items that meet the need for convenience, yet are not excessive in sodium, fat or sugar.

CORPORATE SOCIAL RESPONSIBILITY

The well being of our planet is in the media regularly. Producers and retailers appreciate that their responsibility is to provide food in a manner that will preserve our valuable environment. Sourcing of items is also a focus for retailers as they strive to deliver sustainable products from around the world. **Consumers are becoming much more aware of this issue** and many are demanding more information and transparency in the methods of production and distribution. There is also an increased emphasis on the well being of employees at suppliers and within the retailing network.

PRIORITY ALIGNMENT

Every retailer has its own definition of these various priorities and some would change the level of importance of each to support their own business model. They are focused on these issues to run their business and satisfy the needs of their consumers. Suppliers must incorporate these issues into their own business model. However, the top spot in any priority list must be to increase sales. It is critical to understand where your customer is investing time and resources now and where they intend to in the future. It can take years to develop new items and change processes — that is why it is so important to understand these priorities now and into the future.

Once you have a good understanding of a retailer's priorities, it's important to assess how they relate to your own business priorities. For example: if your customer is focused on a comparable sales increase of 5%, will your item deliver this? If you're unable to deliver the sales increase, will your items be delisted in favour of another supplier who can? Your sales will be impacted either way. It's important to explore each of the priorities as they relate to your customers. They are all focused on each of these issues but they have their own unique perspectives.

In the following chapters we will discuss these priorities in detail. We will explore why they are important to retailers, what they're doing about them and what you as a supplier must do to respond within your own organization. The final chapter will provide a method for you to incorporate these priorities into your own business planning.

This should be such an easy business. The reality is that it is a complex business. Your retail customers own the store so you must understand their needs. They are focused on specific priorities to drive their businesses and bring consumers into the store. You must be aligned with these priorities to meet their needs. In the end, that's what will make your customer a satisfied customer. Satisfied customers generate positive relationships and deliver sales; which is what this is all about!

THREE KEY POINTS TO MAKE SENSE OF A COMPLEX INDUSTRY

1   To be successful, the supplier must satisfy two masters; the customer (who is the retailer) and the ultimate consumer;
    The customer pays a business for a good or service;
    The consumer purchases a product for personal consumption.
2   A successful relationship requires the supplier to be aware of the retailers' priorities;
3   Priorities of the supplier and the retailer must be aligned.

What are your customers' priorities?

_____

_____

_____

_____

_____

What are your business priorities?

_____

_____

_____

_____

_____

_____

CHAPTER 2

SALES ARE
JOB #1 FOR
RETAILERS

WHY SALES ARE SO IMPORTANT

There is no doubt when you work in retail that sales are key. Every morning retail smartphones and emails are alive with daily and weekly updates. Every week there is tremendous focus on the previous week's sales, When I was in retail we would review our performance relative to the same week last year, the budget and the plan. As a supplier you need to respect the retailer's emphasis on sales. You also need to understand how that obsession can have an impact on decision-making in the business. A bad week in sales can lead to immediate changes in advertising retails or item selection.

Sales momentum is critical in retail. If employees working at a retailer are engaged, their mood will change with sales results. Great sales results that deliver numbers above expectations really energize employees. One great aspect of the retail food industry is that you can determine the effectiveness of your plan and your execution very quickly: the cash register will tell you. That's where the shopper votes.

The top line (sales) drives results. In retail, we used to say "volume hides a lot of sins." Each retailer has its own way of describing that, you have to understand that sales are the top priority for your retail customers.

In retail, there are many different metrics to use for analyzing sales results. Retailers review:

Total sales;
Department sales;
Sales per square foot;
Sales per customer;
Sales per labour hour.

These numbers are reviewed for each department and each store. They get scrutinized every week, every month or period and every year. Yes, there is an obsession about sales within retailers.

FIXED COSTS MAKE OR BREAK PROFIT

Many expenses in retail are fixed but if you can achieve volume, these expenses decrease rapidly as a percentage of sales. The store lights are on and people are working no matter whether they do $350,000 or $550,000 per week in a location.

There are, however, many controllable expenses in stores. Labour is the largest controllable expense that retailers have. There are a minimum number of hours required to run a store. When sales start to grow, there are many opportunities to leverage labour and other expenses. Retailers invest considerable resources in finding opportunities to improve their numbers.

When there are more and more opportunities to buy food, food retailers have to be more focused than ever on maintaining and growing sales.

THE RETAIL LANDSCAPE HAS TURNED UPSIDE DOWN

One major challenge facing traditional food retailers is that there are many more, and different, retailers trying to sell food. We once had well defined channels for distribution where grocery stores sold food, pharmacies prescribed medication and sold health care products and department stores sold clothes and household goods. Now they're all trying to be all things to all people. Food stores have pharmacies and clothes, drug stores have sizable percentages of floor space dedicated to food and some mass merchants have more linear feet of food than do some food stores.

Food is a necessary and popular item and it does drive traffic. Traditional food retailers are trying to prevent losing volume to many different stores. The food stores are not innocent in this blurring of channels — they were eager to dive into discounted prescriptions and some even devote considerable space to clothing. No doubt this offers the consumer many one stop shopping options, but it also creates a much more diverse marketplace where the battle to deliver a weekly sales number is more challenging than ever.

The overall retail landscape has evolved and segments within food retailing have gone through significant change as well. The traditional supermarket has evolved into three segments:

Discount food stores;
Conventional (or traditional) food stores;
Large format (or super stores).

The three segments each have a defined target market, however, there's considerable cross shopping. Retailers work diligently every week to put together a program that will entice the consumers to spend their food dollars in their stores.

DISCOUNT FOOD STORES

Discount stores occupy the smallest physical space of the three segments and they rely on high volume and low cost to deliver a bottom line. These stores must be priced competitively and most follow an every day low price program. They price check the competition aggressively and have deeply discounted ads on a select number of items. The discount segment has experienced considerable growth in recent years with the impact of the recession and the changing consumer, driving shoppers into these stores.

CONVENTIONAL (OR TRADITIONAL) FOOD STORES

The physical size of traditional stores is usually between 30,000 sq. ft. and 80,000 sq. ft. and they offer a full array of departments and more service than the other two segments. Pricing is higher with a weekly ad to create excitement, drive traffic and provide a template to support themes and events. Traditional stores have been under more pressure for sales as consumers have shifted away to discount stores to save money. Consumers have also responded to the aggressive real estate expansion program executed by the large stores so the traditional store is caught in the middle, losing to the other formats.

LARGE FORMAT (OR SUPER STORES)

Large stores, which are more than 80,000 sq. ft. have been growing with competitive pricing, one stop shopping and a significant growth in square footage. Walmart, Costco, Real Canadian Superstore, Save On Foods and now Target occupy the large format space. These stores started to open in Canada in the 1980s. They were built as destination stores with the philosophy that consumers would travel up to an hour to shop. This has now changed and you will find them in smaller markets and across the street from each other. They drive considerable traffic and the key for these stores to be successful is delivering value to the customer.

RETAILER'S OBSESSION WITH SALES

Your retail customers work very hard to develop a sales culture. This is done for a number of reasons, which are both internal and external. Internally, employees must be making decisions that will result in consumers making purchases, while externally there is considerable pressure to deliver positive results for shareholders.

The majority of large retailers are publicly traded companies. Sales information is available each quarter and analysts working with the financial institutions put a significant emphasis on the sales numbers reported. Almost everything done by the retailers is determined by sales. This is the first number budgeted and all others are defined as a percentage of sales.

When you see a retailer report financial results, sales are always one of the first metrics to be listed. If sales are not first, they are probably not very encouraging. Retailers report two numbers; absolute and same store (or comparable) sales. Both numbers are important, however, the analysts who assess performance of retailers put a lot of focus on same store sales numbers. The reason that same store sales are so important is that they measure performance in stores that have been open for more than a year. These are the core sales and there is less influence from new retail space through real estate programs or from renovations. Absolute sales are the total sales number for the business.

You should be aware of sales results for your retail customers. These are available in quarterly updates they release which are posted on their websites. Recent results for the major retailers are listed below.

	Absolute sales	Absolute % change	Same store % change
Sobeys Q2 ended November 2, 2013	$4,416,800,000	+2.0%	+0.2%
Metro Q1 ended December 21, 2013	$2,701,300,000	+0.0%	(0.5%)
Loblaw Q3 ended October 5, 2013	$9,772,000,000	+1.5%	+ .4%
Walmart			
U.S.A.	$67,692,000,000	+2.4%	-0.3%
International	$33,109,000,000	+0.2%	n/a
Sam's Club Q3 ended October 31, 2013	$14,075,000,000	+1.1%	n/a
Target Q3 ended November 2, 2013	$17,258,000,000	+4.0%	+0.9%

All sales numbers were taken from results posted on the respective retailer's website.

There are many considerations when comparing sales results. They are not 100% comparable because retailers have different reporting periods. The product mix for each retailer is also different. The Walmart website reports sales with and without gasoline sales due to the fluctuations in pricing. Retailers operating in the United Sates and some Canadian provinces are able to sell alcohol, which is not always part of the product mix. Currency fluctuations also impact sales when they are converted to U.S. dollars for Walmart. Walmart reports sales for the U.S. division, the international division (where Canadian sales are) and the Sam's Club division.

It is always interesting to note the magnitude of sales. Now that Canadian retailers compete directly with Walmart, Target and Costco, you can see the massive sales they compete against. The annual sales of Walmart at $469 billion are daunting. To comprehend the magnitude of these sales, consider them in relation to the economy of entire nations. Using the International Monetary Fund's list of 2012 national gross domestic products, Walmart's 2012 sales would rank #28. Their annual sales are larger than the entire economy of countries such as South Africa, Venezuela and Denmark. It is also interesting to express Walmart sales in relation to the sales of the Canadian retailers:

> Walmart has 16x the annual sales of Loblaw Companies;
> Walmart has 27x the annual sales of Sobeys;
> Walmart has 34x the annual sales of Metro.

If you envision the retailers sitting in a sandbox, which is the Canadian market, Walmart has the magnitude to push the others around.

There are a number of ways retailers generate sales. The most important is location of products on the shelf in the store. Approximately 80% of products are purchased off the regular shelf. With two things necessary for good sales from the shelf; in-stock position and pricing.

Retailers will follow either an every day low pricing philosophy or a high-low strategy.

PRICE CHECKING KEEPS RETAILERS IN THE GAME

Every day low pricing (EDLP) requires a long-term commitment to communicate value. Every day low prices are more consistent and deliver a lower total shopping bill on an average basket of goods. Retailers who subscribe to this do not invest as much in the weekly ad and if possible they would prefer to have no ad at all. Walmart is the best example of an EDLP retailer. It is interesting to note that when the company came to Canada, it had to reduce its dependence on EDLP and invest more in ads to drive traffic. EDLP retailers believe they will get more of the total weekly shop from their loyal shoppers. These consumers need to be convinced they will get the best overall prices. Discount stores also subscribe to this strategy although they do have ads with limited numbers of items at deep discounts.

High-low includes higher shelf prices and deeper discounts in the ads. Conventional food stores usually subscribe to the high-low strategy. Margins are higher on their shelf prices and they offer a wider selection. Ads are designed to drive traffic on impressionable items and often undercut the every day low prices across the street.

Your retail customers put a significant amount of resources into understanding pricing in the market. Retail price checks are done weekly on impressionable items and then a larger list is completed over several weeks. Employees within the merchandising group devote hours to reviewing the price checks and working to ensure they are priced properly within the market. It is very important you understand the price of your items at the various retailers. If you're in a highly price sensitive category and one retailer makes a change, you need to understand the impact on the rest of your retail customers. They will notice it!

PRICE CHECKING ESPIONAGE

The entrance of Price Club (subsequently converted to Costco in Canada) was a challenge for traditional retailers for many reasons. We were faced with a competitor that charged consumers a membership fee, operated on lower margins and had unique sizes and products. They would not let the other retailers in to price check the stores. We had no way to get reliable information about pricing to ensure we were competitive.

We had to resort to some price checking espionage to get the information we needed. Our merchandising employees were dispatched to stores with a mini tape recorder and strict instructions to destroy the tape if accosted by an employee. We would walk the aisles and recite item and price into our sleeves, which contained the cleverly hidden mini recorders. Only a small number of our employees were asked to leave, but we got the information we needed to keep our stores competitive.

RETAILERS ARE ADDICTED TO ADS

Ads are another vehicle used by retailers to generate traffic and drive sales. Millions are invested each week to produce ads, not to mention the investment in gross profit through reduced prices. Since the recession, we have seen consumers put even more emphasis on the items in the flyers when do-

ing their weekly shopping. In A.C. Nielsen's "State of the Industry" they report that 36% of sales and 48% of tonnage are items with temporary price reductions. Ads will drive incremental volume. Retailers will create a grid of items months in advance and specific item selection will happen six to eight weeks in advance of the flyer being in effect.

Retailers will react to the current market place swiftly. If sales are disappointing, consumers can be attracted the very next day with strong item and price ads. Often we were called upon to drop what we were doing and react to a newspaper ad for the very next day.

SOFT D_INKS

Christmas is a critical time for food retailers. Consumers are in the mood to spend and they are willing to buy many items that do not sell the rest of the year. It is critical to generate traffic during week 51, the week prior to Christmas. In the 90's we would run full-page newspaper ads to generate traffic during these key weeks. Today, digital files are transmitted over the Internet, but we would send physical artwork to the newspapers to create plates and print ads.

I was responsible for marketing and advertising across Atlantic Canada at the time. The merchandising department confirmed they would invest thousands of dollars to advertise 2L pop at .99 per bottle. This was a significant investment, one that was sure to drive customers in to our stores like bees to honey. A critical ad during the important holiday season in the competition to bring in consumers. You can imagine my horror when the ads ran in every market with the missing "r" from the word "drinks." It was a memorable ad for a lot more than a great price on pop.

SERVICE LEVEL IS MORE THAN A NUMBER

Execution throughout the retailer's business is a key to driving sales. Products must flow through the supply chain and get to the shelf at the right price. Themes and ads must be effectively merchandised. There are many factors related to execution that will deliver sales. Retailers have operations supervisors who are tasked with making sure execution is as good as it should be.

Service level is a measurement that's reviewed daily as it has a direct effect on sales. If product is not getting to the warehouse, through the warehouse, or to the store, sales will suffer. Store level ordering will also impact service level. A 5% drop in service level can result in a sales decline of 1%.

Retailers rely on themes, holidays and events to drive sales. These opportunities can be key in delivering incremental sales growth. A significant amount of resources are devoted to getting the ads right on key weeks and helping stores order items they only see once per year (such as fruitcake or mini Easter eggs).

There are many different drivers of sales. Each retailer has its own philosophy of which is most effective and why. Suppliers must understand where each retailer is putting the focus and how they can contribute.

SUPPLIERS NEED TO BE OBSESSED WITH SALES

To ensure your business is aligned with your customer's priorities, you need to get focused on sales and sell-through at retail. Foster a culture of sales reporting and challenge employees to know their sales numbers, keep them front and centre.

Sales success at retail is like climbing a mountain. The first step, the listing, is only base camp, the warehouse is level one, and the rest of the climb to the summit of driving sales is dependent on great planning and execution.

The retailers define sales as items going through the cash register. Do your sales people know what the sell-through of your product should be and what it actually is? Focus on sales as products get into the shopping cart, not when they go in the warehouse.

SUBSCRIBE TO THE PHILOSOPHY THAT PRODUCTS ARE SOLD WHEN THEY GO IN THE SHOPPING CART AND THROUGH THE CASH REGISTER AT THE STORE.

Your business and your retail customers should have the same definition of the sales plan. I have worked with many suppliers who were intimidated to talk about sales. This is one of the most important topics for you to discuss with the retailer. Every year you should both agree on what the potential volume is and how you will achieve these results. Your success will be defined in large part by the program you implement and the sales your item achieves. You must have the same expectations as the retailer.

DO YOU HAVE A PLAN?

Define your sales in terms of your customers. Overall, sales by customer is vital. Which items are growing with each of your retailers will tell you a lot about where the focus needs to be and also which programs are successful. One other measure of sales worth exploring is sales per store. If you sell 5,000 cases per year and the retailer has 135 stores then you are doing less than one case per week per store. Every department and every category has different sales expectations, however, less than one case per week per store could be a problem.

Understand your sales performance relative to your retail customer's performance. The numbers reported are only for the total business. You will need to do some research to understand your department or your category. Retailers are very secretive about sales details. In your meetings with category managers you need to ask questions about sales. They will be reluctant to give you actual sales numbers other than those publicly reported, but you should ask if your item(s) are performing at the category growth or above/below. It is important you know these facts; it should help you build your programs with the retailers.

Year over year sales growth is critical. You need to know when ads were run in the previous year and how it affected volume. Retailers will be looking to meet or exceed those numbers so you must be prepared and be proactive if possible. Remind them of the programs that delivered sales and figure out a mutually beneficial program to repeat successes. They have many items, categories and regions to manage, do not ever assume they will remember everything that worked.

WHEN YOU HAVE A PLAN, TALK ABOUT IT

The biggest win for your business is to bring sales opportunities to the retailers. You should always include these in your meetings with category managers. What do you have that could help them meet or exceed their sales numbers? Every time you meet with the category manager you should include sales as a topic and bring ideas forward. Your ideas might not always get accepted, but at least the retailer will know you are focused on sales.

Every item needs a sales plan and it's effective to share components of the plan with your retail customers. They will have much more faith in your abilities when you outline your plans for the item. Always remember that it is your job to sell the items, not the retailer's. Retailers provide a store and a shopping cart for the consumer, you need to provide the incentive for the shopper in the store to pick up the item and make the decision to buy. Your sales plan should be an annual plan that addresses all of the opportunities to get your item into the shopping cart of the consumer. Too many suppliers see success as getting an item listed or delivered to the warehouse. This is only part of the process. Sales through the cash register need to be generated every week, every year.

There are many tactics available to achieve sales success. Determine which are the most effective tactics for your particular item and in your category. You must select the options that are effective and affordable within your business plan.

DO YOU KNOW WHAT YOUR IN-STOCK POSITION IS?

The most important component of the sales plan is how you will sell the items off the regular shelf. Approximately 80% of product sales occur off the regular shelf, that is where the item is every day, every week. Your item must be in stock and whenever possible have a sign, signs sell! You must invest some resources to ensure your shelf presence is as good as it can be. Most retailers implement plan-o-grams that determine the shelf placement for every item. The purpose of plan-o-grams is to provide the store employees with the correct alignment of items to drive sales and deliver profit. Plan-o-grams are usually created in the merchandising group using information from suppliers. All items within the category are considered and placement is based on a number of factors; including sales, profit, size, private label stock keeping units (SKUs) in the category, listing fees and complimentary items.

When your item is listed it will be inserted in the plan-o-gram and that's the signal for the store to reline the shelf with new items. Suppliers should always know where the item is in the plan-o-gram and follow up at the store level to ensure execution. A new item with great potential will never sell if it's not put in the correct place on the shelf.

Retailers use this process to ensure consistency and allow them to analyze results. It is critical for suppliers to check to see items are on the shelf and communicate back to the merchandisers with the positive or negative results. Stores have hundreds of four-foot sections to manage and you will probably have to talk to people at the store level and perhaps the merchandising department to get execution across all stores. It is not possible to visit all stores so you might have to enlist the services of a retail broker or merchandiser. If the plan-o-gram does not get changed your item may not get ordered and sales will fall short of expectations.

ANY CHANCE TO GET A SIGN? THEY SELL.

The priority in selling off the shelf is to have the item available for sale. The second priority is to determine if there are any in-store pricing programs or signage opportunities that will prompt the sales of your item. Most retailers employ these tools to drive some incremental sales. Visit the stores and determine which tools would be effective for your products and in your categories. Often retailers with preferred customer programs offer incremental signage for participating products. Signage sells products, therefore, a slight retail price reduction with a sign can drive some strong sales.

A very powerful in-store option for driving sales is the product demonstration or demo. This is an opportunity for the consumer to try to the product right at the point of purchase. This is probably the most effective tactic to sell product; it's also one of the most expensive options. Many retailers have their own demo programs they manage and coordinate, while others will allow you to do your own demos. Explore the options and make sure the timing is right. If your item is a great BBQ product, a Friday afternoon in the heat of the summer would be perfect. Even better if you've managed to arrange it for a sunny day!

The weekly flyer is an integral part of the retailer's promotion strategy. You will need to propose ad opportunities several months ahead to ensure your items are considered. There is always a lot of emphasis on the front page items, but do not lose sight of the opportunities an inside item can have. Watch the ads every week and look for themes where you could participate. Often, lower selling items will be grouped together to provide the retailer with the sales levels required to warrant the space in the ad. Obviously it's the retailer's decision as to what goes in the ad but you should have a plan for how many ads will benefit your item and work to achieve those ad positions.

COUPONS — THEY'RE BACK!

Coupons have been a promotion tool for a long time to provide incentive for trial or purchase. Their popularity seems to ebb and flow, however, they remain popular, especially when a consumer's discretionary income is tight. Most retailers have specific regulations about the coupons they can redeem, so make sure you understand the program. You cannot just put coupons on your website and expect the retailers to honour them, even if you are prepared to pay for the redemption. Follow the correct process and the retailer will appreciate the investment you are making in your product.

There are a number of options available outside the store that will drive sales as well. Traditional mass media advertising can create demand for your item and awareness for your brand. There are many new social media platforms to choose from as well. No matter what you choose, communicate it to your retail customers. They need to see you are making an investment in your items. Since there could be implications for sales, they might want to adjust inventory levels to accommodate increases.

When you create your sales plan you should anticipate the seasonality of the item. There are few if any items that sell the same every week. Your sales plan should reflect the changes in volume and, if possible, implement some tactics to deliver sales in non-traditional times. An example of this is when the dairies bring eggnog out for a limited four week program in the summer. An item that is usually only available at Christmas can generate some incremental volume in the summer.

There are many different methods of driving sales and you must find the best results and the most cost effective ideas for your items. You must have a plan to sell your item; the retailer will not do this for you. Sales are their #1 priority and they will achieve their goals with the items that deliver the desired results in their stores.

RESPECT THE SYSTEMS AND PROCESSES THAT ALLOW THE RETAILERS TO OPERATE BUT NEVER LOSE SIGHT OF HOW IMPORTANT RELATIONSHIPS ARE TO YOUR BUSINESS.

It is important to share components of your strategy to drive sales with your customers. You need to have a shared opinion of what the potential sales are for different items. This is critical as you assess performance and determine options for the future.

THREE KEY POINTS TO DRIVE SALES

1. Develop a sales culture within your business;
2. Every item needs a sales plan — the retailer will not do this for you;
3. Discuss sales numbers with retailers to ensure you both have a similar expectation for results. This should be done at least three times per year.

How can you drive sales?

_____

_____

_____

_____

_____

_____

CHAPTER 3

DIFFERENTIATE TO SURVIVE

THE DOG EAT DOG WORLD OF FOOD RETAILING

The retail landscape is getting more cluttered all the time. Everyone wants to sell food and it is tougher than ever to stand out from the crowd. It's a challenge to find meaningful differences from one store to another. Our market is so competitive that a unique point of differentiation does not last for long. To understand where we are it is interesting to explore the journey we have been on.

In the '80's, we were listening to disco and watching E.T. Our Canadian food landscape was dominated by traditional food stores. Approximately 70% of the food market in Canada was conducted in conventional food stores. There were a few super centres in the market operated by Loblaw and discount chains that were getting more attention. Discount stores started as low cost alternatives in locations where conventional food stores did not perform well. The idea was to strip out costs and reduce losses or turn it in to a modest profit. Consumers embraced the idea and sales blossomed.

THE RETAIL LANDSCAPE IN THE 1980'S

LARGE STORE	TRADITIONAL STORE		DISCOUNT
Real Canadian Superstore	Safeway	Sobeys	Price Chopper
Costco	Metro IGA	Steinberg's	No Frills
Save On Foods	Co-op	Dominion	Food Basics
	Loblaws	Zehrs	Extra Foods
	Fortinos	Provigo	
	Atlantic Superstore		
	Save Easy	Overwaitea	
10% of total market	**70% of total market**		**20% of total market**

I will always remember the day in January 1994, when we were called into the boardroom at our Loblaw office to hear the news that Walmart was coming to Canada. The dark cloudy day and weather outside reflected the mood inside. We all knew it was eventually going to happen but reality is different. Nobody would ever admit it, but we felt like we were the people living in a country where war had just been declared. The result is inevitable but no one has the courage to say what challenges lay ahead. We would put on a brave face and say 'competition is good for everyone' but we knew our working life would never be the same. At Loblaws we would not be the biggest kid in the sand box for long.

Walmart's acquisition of Woolco in 1994 still has an impact on our Canadian retail landscape.

The food industry was familiar with Walmart's march across the U.S. from region to region; taking food business from all of the traditional retail giants such as Kroger and Safeway. The Canadian stores opened with very little food but we always knew it was in the plan. Walmart's first pantry stores opened with as much linear footage of grocery, dairy and frozen as a traditional food store. The battle for the consumer's food dollar suddenly became more intense than ever in markets where Walmart was competing.

Aside from Walmart there were other changes that occurred in the '90's. Steinberg's stores were dismantled in Quebec and Dominion stores in Ontario struggled under the ownership of A&P. Loblaw was expanding and became a national retailer with the acquisition of Provigo in 1998. Sobeys was also expanding outside its traditional Atlantic Canadian roots with the bold acquisition of the Oshawa Group (IGA & Foodland in Ontario and Western Canada) in 1998.

THE RETAIL LANDSCAPE IN THE 1990'S

LARGE STORE	TRADITIONAL STORE		DISCOUNT	
Real Canadian Superstore	Safeway	Sobeys	Price Chopper	
Costco	Metro	IGA	No Frills	Maxi & Co.
Save On Foods	Co op	Dominion	Food Basics	
Walmart	Loblaws	Zehrs	Extra Foods	
	Fortinos	Provigo	Super C (Metro)	
	Your Independent Grocer			
	Atlantic Superstore		PriceSmart Foods	
	Save Easy	Overwaitea		
15% of total market	**60% of total market**		**25% of total market**	

The following decade experienced less consolidation, however, the shift from traditional food stores to large stores and discount continued. Costco continued to expand and Walmart was opening super centers in Ontario and Western Canada. Large cavernous stores were beginning to draw shoppers from smaller more intimate food stores. The dollars transacted in large stores and discount segments became very close to the traditional food stores.

We also saw the entry of some specialty stores in response to a changing consumer. The T&T chain opened in Western Canada, and was subsequently purchased by Loblaw Companies and Whole Foods entered the Ontario market. Giant Tiger started to become a player in the food market with a limited offering and low prices.

THE RETAIL LANDSCAPE IN THE 2000'S

LARGE STORE	TRADITIONAL STORE		DISCOUNT	
Real Canadian Superstore	Safeway	Sobeys	Price Chopper	FreshCo
Costco	Metro	IGA	No Frills	Maxi & Co.
Save On Foods	Co op	Whole Foods	Food Basics	
Walmart	Loblaws	Zehrs	Extra Foods	
	Fortinos	Provigo	Super C (Metro)	
	Your Independent Grocer		Giant Tiger	
	Atlantic Superstore	T&T	PriceSmart Foods	
	Save Easy	Overwaitea		
20% of total market	**50% of total market**		**30% of total market**	

Our Canadian landscape today continues to evolve. Sobeys' acquisition of Safeway and Loblaw's acquisition of Shoppers Drug Mart in 2013 brought consolidation back to the forefront. Consumers continue to have more large stores to choose from with Target opening 125 stores across Canada and with Walmart super centers now open in every region. Costco is moving into smaller markets and Loblaw has No Frills stores in every region.

THE LANDSCAPE IS CHANGING

Recently I was shopping with my daughters. We were looking for some snacks to include in their lunch for summer camp. Shopping with two girls under eight years old can be a challenge, especially in the snack aisle when they are hungry. It is amazing how many items you can reach even when you are in the shopping cart. A woman noticed us looking for fruit cups – which were out of stock – and pulled me aside. In a hushed voice she told me "they are much cheaper at Giant Tiger and they have plenty."

The most valuable advertising is word of mouth and the discount chain was getting it from this shopper. She was pretty much telling me to load the kids in the car and get over to Giant Tiger. Shopping for food is not the same for consumers or retailers as it was 15 years ago. The shopper continues to embrace the value offered in large stores and low prices of discount banners. Traditional food stores have higher costs and lower volume; a dilemma for these stores. Square footage is growing in the large stores and also in discount segments, making it even more convenient than ever for consumers to leave conventional stores.

THE RETAIL LANDSCAPE IN 2014

LARGE STORE	TRADITIONAL STORE	DISCOUNT
Real Canadian Superstore	IGA Sobeys	Price Chopper FreshCo
Costco	Metro	No Frills Maxi & Co.
Save On Foods	Co op Whole Foods	Food Basics
Walmart	Loblaws Zehrs	Extra Foods
Target	Fortinos Provigo	Super C (Metro)
	Your Independent Grocer	Giant Tiger
	Atlantic Superstore T&T	PriceSmart Foods
	Save Easy Overwaitea	
25% of total market	**40% of total market**	**35% of total market**

We also have other retail channels selling food. Drug stores are full of food and even Canadian Tire has some food available. Despite food being in many stores, consumers still have to visit one of the large stores, traditional food stores or discount food stores to complete a full shop. It is important to remember any dollar that is lost to a

store such as Canadian Tire puts more strain on food retailers. Their costs remain the same and if volume declines, working for a food retailer or being a supplier becomes as much fun as a spoon full of spicy sauce on ice cream.

A retailer's strategy to differentiate is developed with a number of components. Store formats, control label, selection, execution and labour all have an impact on differentiation. The right mix, well executed can be the difference between success and failure.

> UNDERSTAND THE COMPETITIVE ENVIRONMENT IN WHICH THEY OPERATE. LET THEM DO THEIR JOB AND REMEMBER YOU ARE ONE OF MANY.

THE FORMAT IS THE BRAND

Store formats are essentially the brand for retailers. Consumers have a perception of what the format or brand will deliver and that is a key factor in their decision as to where they shop. Retailers invest significant money and resources into creating and operating their formats. Shopping experience, pricing, ads, product mix and execution all determine positioning and perception of the format.

Suppliers must understand the offering in each format and develop opportunities to satisfy these expectations.

Store formats may all be selling food but they are each unique. This is similar to my three children, all growing up in the same community and the same school, yet each has a unique personality. Each child has a different focus and a set of currencies that are important to them. My son loves sports and is very passionate about competing and participating. My eldest daughter is our princess. She is happiest doing crafts and playing with her stuffed animals. The youngest is full of personality with a zest for life. All fantastic children, but each unique. As they get older they will change over the years. It is important to think of your retail customers in the same light. They may all sell food but each has its own unique strategy to accomplish this.

DEVELOP A UNIQUE STRATEGY FOR EACH RETAILER.

Retailers compete with their formats and their own strategy. Some retailers operate a multi banner strategy such as Loblaw, which competes in every segment. Other retailers such as Costco have one format they put in every market. The product mix might be slightly different but overall they are very similar. The following table illustrates how larger retailers in Canada are entrenched in the market:

	LARGE STORE	TRADITIONAL FOOD STORE	DISCOUNT	SPECIALTY STORE	DRUG
Loblaw	Real Canadian Superstore	Loblaws Zehrs Fortinos Your Independent Grocer Atlantic Superstore Save Easy Provigo	No Frills Maxi & Co. Extra Foods	T&T	Shoppers Drug Mart In-store pharmacy
Sobeys		Sobeys Safeway Foodland IGA	FreshCo Price Chopper		Lawtons In-store pharmacy
Metro	Super C	Metro	Food Basics	Adonis	In-store pharmacy
Pattison Group	Save On Foods	Overwaitea	PriceSmart Foods		In-store pharmacy
Target	Target				In-store pharmacy
Walmart	Walmart Super Centre		Walmart pantry		In-store pharmacy
Costco	Costco				In-store pharmacy

PRICING IS KING

The simplest way for retailers to differentiate banners or formats is through pricing. This can be quantified and we have done a great job training the consumer to watch for lower prices.

Discount banners have the lowest prices, then large stores, with the highest prices in traditional food stores. There is a direct correlation between the level of pricing and tangible expenses such as labour, store fixtures and shrink. The higher the gross profit, these become more affordable. The real winners are stores that deliver a great shopping experience (as defined by their customer) and value.

The most important factor in the success of Loblaw's No Frills banner was the quality of the perishables. They once had the best prices but had been synonymous with poor quality fresh items. When they did a superior job of execution, consumers rewarded them at the cash register. Consumers were not willing to pay lower prices for rotting vegetables, however, they would fill their cart with quality smaller apples at a lower price.

Retailers use a weighted average to compare prices from one banner to another. They know their own product mix and use price checks done at all stores to create a shopping basket. Consumers will not notice a difference of less than 5% but when the gap starts to widen, sales will either grow or decline.

Retailers invest significant resources to keep pricing in line with the market. They appreciate suppliers who understand their pricing platforms and those who deliver opportunities to support the positioning of their banner(s).

LISTING BASE IS THE PERSONALITY OF THE STORE

There are many ways to sell the same item in a food store. I recall counting pizza in one location and we had more than 50 SKUs in five different departments. That's a lot of pizza! Needless to say, we had the pizza customer covered. The offering for consumers should support the positioning of the format. We investigated the offerings and we found several SKUs really did not support the positioning of the format and did not differentiate our offering.

Shelf space, and more importantly refrigerated and frozen shelf space, is at a premium. Category managers must manage their listing base to maximize sales and gross profit while supporting the positioning of the banner or format. There are many different ways to sell the same item. The challenge for the merchandisers is to find offerings that will deliver results and differentiate the banner. Suppliers who bring products forward that deliver this are worth a lot more than those who bring the same product to every retailer and every banner. Changes as subtle as pack size or the store labour required can make the difference.

Different departments have different opportunities to differentiate. Fresh departments or perishable departments have the greatest opportunities. There are different ways to sell ketchup but at the end of the day it is still ketchup. In the grocery department there are different sizes or formats (such as squeezable bottles) but they are limited. Fresh departments can be as diverse as full service deli items and prepackaged ready to serve deli items.

Exponential growth of prepared foods offerings has brought significant opportunities for retailers to differentiate in these departments. Full meal offerings at a traditional retailer such as Sobeys or Loblaw are very different than the pre-cooked BBQ chicken and prepared salads at a discount store. Costco has carved out a unique offering in prepared foods with a limited menu that delivers great value. I can recall certain Loblaw employees who found it hard to do a store visit to Costco without stopping for a $1 hot dog or soft serve ice cream. These items really reinforce Costco's positioning in the market. Value for lunch keeps the shoppers in the stores.

The produce department is where there are many opportunities to differentiate. One of the biggest is size. Not all apples grow to an 88 size. Discount retailers will sell the smaller produce and traditional food stores will sell larger apples. Larger, more mature fruit should have a better natural sugar content and more flavour. Large super stores will sell more packaged produce to convey value.

Selection available in the perishable departments is another form of differentiation. In a full service produce department there can be more than 500 SKUs where as a discount store might only have 250 SKUs. The business model is that more items bring more customers. However, prices need to be higher to support the shrink that will occur with greater selection. Sales in a department such as produce drop off very rapidly after you get through the top 25 items. In a full service produce department, bananas account for approximately 10% of the entire department's weekly sales, which means they are close to 1% of store sales. Bananas are the largest single selling SKU in the store.

THERE IS NOTHING PRIVATE ABOUT PRIVATE LABEL

Every major retailer operating in Canada has a control label or private label program. The words control label and private label are synonymous to retailers. There are a number of reasons they operate control label programs:

1 Margins are higher on these items;
2 These products are loyalty programs. If a consumer prefers a President's Choice product from Loblaw they have to go back to Loblaw to get it;
3 Control label is one of the few unique aspects of the shopping experience. A delicious chocolate dessert or a unique Asian cooking sauce with an authentic kick can entice people to the store. Once retailers get them in the door, it is much easier to fill the shopping cart.

Most retailers operate different levels of control label programs. One might be designed to offer value relative to the national brands while one is designed to be unique and support traditional food store positioning.

Every retailer has their own philosophy about control label products. Some view them as an integral part of the offering. Others view them as an opportunity for some extra margin or because it is a perceived gap if they do not have it. It is necessary to understand and respect the control label programs. Retailers can perceive a product that competes with one of theirs as a threat. Some of the best insights into control label philosophy are at the store. Retailers can say they are dedicated to it but where is it merchandised at the store? If the products are on the bottom shelf and collecting dust they are not dedicated. It is also interesting to ask store employees about control label products. If there is true commitment they will understand the items and be excited about them.

This table illustrates the control label food products sold in each Canadian retailer.

	FOODIE ITEMS	UNIQUE	VALUE	HEALTH & WELLNESS	GLOBAL FOODS	ORGANIC	SUSTAINABILITY
Loblaw	PC Black	President's Choice	No Name	PC Blue Menu	T&T	PC Organic	PC Green
Sobeys	Sensations	Compliments	Signal	Compliments Balance		Compliments Organics	Compliments Greencare
Metro		Irresistibles	Selection				
Walmart		Our Finest	Great Value				
Costco			Kirkland				
Target		Archer Farms	Market Pantry				
Whole Foods		365					
Overwaitea		Western Family				Western Family Organics	

Loblaw has one of the strongest, if not the strongest control label program in Canada. One of the best parts of my job at Loblaw was when we had the opportunity to participate in President's Choice product development. The merchandisers from the different regions would come together to meet at the PC test kitchen in Brampton. This is a phenomenal facility full of every ingredient and every kitchen appliance you can imagine. Bakery was my favourite. I was fortunate to participate in the development of several tasty PC dessert items. Can you imagine walking in to a room with eight versions of hot, gooey PC chocolate molten lava cakes? We would have to try several of these items and rate them on different product attributes. (It's a tough job but someone has to do it.)

The President's Choice program was implemented by one of the most influential people in Canadian food retailing; Dave Nichol. He was passionate about President's Choice and his expectation was that everyone around him would have the same passion. His tirades were famous within

Loblaw. He would select certain items, such as PC Memories of Szechuan peanut sauce, that he perceived to be great opportunities for sales and differentiation. His dedication and persistence would force execution, which resulted in items with no sales moving to the top of the category. Each one designed to reinforce a point of differentiation only available at Loblaw stores. He left the company in the mid 90's to pursue other interests. He was never as successful after leaving Loblaw and he passed away in 2013. A great lesson in retailing, the power is not as much the individual but the position of controlling the shelf space.

DEMOS WITH DAVE NICHOL

Dave Nichol was well known for his passion for President's Choice. In Atlantic Canada we did not get a lot of exposure to him in our market. His work was in Toronto but on one occasion we learned he was coming down to speak at the University of Prince Edward Island. A few of us were dispatched to get the local store looking good and add a little extra PC signage in anticipation of his visit. We also secured some people to do demos of PC products in the store.

During his tour of the store he stopped at one of the demos and asked the man serving the PC lasagna, "what do you think of the product?" The person doing the demo replied, "I haven't tried it, usually I sample for Kraft." We braced ourselves for a verbal assault but he just looked at us and smiled. He knew we had more to learn.

It is becoming more popular to conduct events to support or emphasize control label products. Loblaw has its Insider's Report that is distributed quarterly and Sobeys has the Inspired program. These are significant initiatives to drive differentiation. It is expensive to develop items, produce point of sale signage, print booklets and re-merchandise stores. These events command a lot of resources and they are very high profile within the retailers.

When I was at Loblaw we used to talk about control label in terms of "getting religion" which is another way to say "you have to buy in." Sometimes it is easier to take money from a national brand for prime shelf space. If you have true commitment to control label you leave money on the table and put your own product in the best spot. Long term, differentiation is more important than the short-term infusion of money.

ENTERTAIN CONSUMERS TO MAKE SHOPPING FUN

In-store events are great opportunities to reinforce the positioning of the banner and differentiate the offering. Suppliers should understand the events offered at different stores. Retailers make significant investments to create these events; therefore, it's worth the effort to support these initiatives. Keep in mind this is the retailer talking to their customers.

Events take on many different faces. The most common events support seasonal initiatives such as Easter, Canada Day, Halloween and Christmas. Depending on the banner and market, it's becoming more common to see events created to celebrate holidays from many different cultures. This will continue to grow as the face of our consumer changes. Holiday events are common from one retailer to another. Items are usually close and the real point of differentiation is store execution.

Every retailer has events that are unique to them. These unique events are real opportunities for suppliers. Participation is perceived to be a show of support and more of a partnership. At the end of the day, both retailers and suppliers want to sell product, but these unique events are different. They are different because this is the retailer trying to differentiate its store from the one across the street.

There is a significant amount of planning that goes into creating merchandising events. The work will start months ahead and depending on lead-time for items, plans are finalized at least four weeks prior to the event happening. It takes coordination to procure items, build merchandising plans, develop point of sale signage and most importantly get the stores excited.

Event merchandising has become a critical part of the retailer's strategy to differentiate the banners. These are opportunities to create sales opportunities. It is incredible to think that one football game in late January will give North Americans an excuse to consume chicken wings, chips and pop for days. The Super Bowl is a great example of event merchandising that will drive sales.

Retailers are creatures of habit. A successful event will be executed year after year until it runs its course. Watch the stores and the calendar. If there is an event that has potential for your products, start to work on plans a year in advance and get the calendar from your customer to participate.

EVENTS CAN MAKE YOUR YEAR

In-store events should be monitored just like pricing. Keep a calendar of events and watch for sales opportunities. These events are planned months in advance so it is critical for suppliers to get options on the table early.

Merchandising events are designed to build traffic and create incremental sales. These events can be the difference between making a sales budget and missing it. Off shelf displays with Point of Sale (POS) signage that entice consumers to spend money are a great thing.

It's not possible to support every event, suppliers would go broke. Determine which are right for the items and the business. At times it is strategically important to keep your competition out.

Retailers check their competition frequently so remember to spread out the investment: you can expect a call if you declined to participate in one customer's Chinese New Year but show up across the street. This does not mean you have to be everything to everybody but be prepared for the question. You must keep your investment consistent with the different customers as a percentage of sales and find the most effective vehicles at each retailer to deliver desired results.

SHOPPING EXPERIENCE IS THE ULTIMATE ATTRIBUTE

The shopping experience in store is crucial to the positioning of banners or formats. Of any of the attributes we have discussed, this is the most subjective. One shopper might like the look and feel of a Sobeys whereas another might be drawn to the market style stores Loblaw has been building.

Retailers spend a lot of time trying to define their target market. Once this is done they must build and execute stores designed to satisfy the needs of these consumers. Store design and fixtures play an important role in communicating positioning of the banner. These decisions have a direct impact on the investment in store and on the profit required to sustain the banner. Stores with expensive fixtures sitting on valuable real state must deliver a higher rate of return. Beautiful stores are only part of the mix as long as they contribute a profit.

Discount stores are designed to look cheap as it is part of the banner positioning. Simple fixtures and concrete walls communicate low prices to shoppers.

Colour will play a role in the positioning of stores as well. Loblaw has invested millions to convince people when they see banana yellow at No Frills that prices are lower.

The investment stores make in labour has a direct impact on the shopping experience. More hours cost more money, however, quality and level of service are important variables. The more staff available, the better the quality should appear to be. They are able to cull shelves and counters more frequently and keep great product available for sale. Consumers will pay more for better quality relative to other banners.

Quality of the service is important too. Many consumers really don't like to do grocery shopping. For most, the faster they can get in and out, the better. But one aspect is common – when they want to check out, they don't want to wait. More checkouts open and staff available helps ease the burden of shopping.

EXECUTION WILL BRING THEM BACK

One of the biggest impediments in the way of differentiation for retailers is execution at store level. The best-laid plans are all in vain if stores do not execute. Execution is the result of many things:

1. Great planning;
2. Robust systems;
3. Strong processes;
4. Sound data integrity;
5. Service level;
6. Effective merchandising fixtures at retail;
7. Engaged employees.

The first six points on my list are the result of a strong organization or they can be purchased. Understand where each of your customers has strengths and weaknesses on this list. They are all unique and suppliers must develop programs and plans to support these strengths and weaknesses. For example: if your customer is dedicated to planning 12 months out, then you must be ready for this timetable and get in front of their schedule.

Finding quality employees who are willing to stand for an eight-hour shift, work any day of the week and be compensated with minimum wage is more difficult than ever. We used to look at the employee base in a store or department and define them as warm bodies or real workers. Finding engaged part-time employees is a great accomplishment.

ENGAGED EMPLOYEES WHO EXECUTE ARE VERY VALUABLE.

Working in retail is also becoming more complex than ever. Stores carry a more diverse array of items and no one wants to have a customer ask you a question you can't answer. Staff are expected to understand new items, execute merchandising plans, operate equipment and perhaps even operate a cooking school. Retailers expect a lot.

Recently, I had the opportunity to attend a cooking class at one of the retailers' community rooms. It was in the evening so perhaps the staff had been working all day but it was obvious there were many places they would rather be. They could not be less engaged in serving the customers and making it an enjoyable experience. We learned how to make the recipe but the atmosphere was very flat. By contrast the following day I was on a store tour and the manager and other employees could not have been more engaged. What a difference great employees can make.

SUPPLIERS ARE CRITICAL IN DIFFERENTIATION

Suppliers play a very important role in differentiating retailers. People are in these stores to purchase products that are created and produced by suppliers. The store and employees are the vehicle to get the items to consumers; ergo, the products are critical.

It is so powerful for suppliers to develop products and programs to support positioning of the banners.

The first thing suppliers must do is understand the formats of their customer. They have different stores for a reason. All product attributes should be reviewed to ensure they meet the criteria to support positioning of the banner. Sales, marketing, product development and production should have a solid understanding of the difference between an item for a large store, a traditional food store and a discount store. If we review the traditional 4 P's of marketing it is apparent one product should be offered in different options to support banner positioning.

	PRODUCT	PRICE	PLACE	PROMOTION
Large store	Larger size for value Middle of the road ingredients for price	Value	Most shelf space available	Flyer Shelf pricing program Space for full pallets
Traditional food store	Higher end Interesting ingredients Unique Best for seasonal items	Highest per unit	Best choice of fixtures More labour intensive Full service perishables	Theme ads Events High-low flyer program Locked in shelf pricing End caps
Discount store	Size to hit a price point Lowest cost of production	Lowest per unit	Simple fixtures Limited refrigeration No labour at retail Case cut	EDLP Flyer with low retail Pallet ready displays

Suppliers who follow this philosophy will have the greatest chance for success. Visit the stores of your customers and walk the store with a shopping cart. See the store as a consumer sees it. Challenge everyone in the organization to ensure items are the right fit for consumers and formats.

THE PRICE IS RIGHT IS MORE THAN A GAME SHOW

Retailers are preoccupied with pricing, suppliers should be too. Every time a cost is presented to a retailer, suppliers should have a very good idea where they will set the retail. Use history and category margin estimates to predict regular pricing and ad pricing.

The retailer's different formats have different category and department margin budgets. A discount store only needs to make 20% melded margin in grocery where as a traditional food store will need 26%. When determining product cost and size, consider these different parameters.

It is the retailer's job to price items but suppliers need to know where it will be. Suppliers must provide a cost that will get items priced at a retail that will sell at regular price and in ad. There also must be reasonable profit for suppliers and retailers.

Suppliers should monitor ads and do price checks regularly. It takes 15 minutes to scan ads each week and the best thing about regular price checks is that it gets supplier's employees in stores. Ads can be reviewed online from anywhere. Depending on the category and volatility of pricing, it might only be necessary to check shelf retails every four weeks.

It is imperative for suppliers to know what is happening with pricing in categories where they compete. It also reinforces to category managers that the supplier sees the issue as important.

THE SHOE DOES NOT FIT THE SAME IN EVERY STORE

One of the most common mistakes from suppliers is the assumption that every one of their items is a great opportunity in every store. There is no doubt that one person will want that item, but will it generate the volume to earn the space on shelf?

Retailers have much more respect for suppliers who put together programs that include only items that will sell in each of their stores. It is much more productive to focus the conversation on true opportunities as opposed to sorting through items that are not the right fit.

The best place to do this is the store. Make a list of items in the category and determine where items will fit. It is important to understand national brand and control label offerings in the category. If you are going to displace an item it will be the branded product. In a small category with an established private label option it is probably better to look elsewhere.

A good exercise is to put yourself in the position of category manager. The shelf is not getting any bigger so: what do you suggest comes out or gets reduced facings to make room for your new item?

TO BE OR NOT TO BE — A CONTROL LABEL SUPPLIER

One of the most common questions I get asked by suppliers is "should I produce control label products?"

There are definite advantages and disadvantages to this strategy. It is critical for suppliers to have a clearly defined strategic plan which should determine the direction for the business. If the plan is to build a brand then control label could be a distraction, whereas if plant volume and efficiency are critical, then control label could be an important component.

The advantages to producing control label are:
1. Production volume;
2. Builds your relationship with retailer;
3. Control label suppliers are more important;
4. Reduces marketing and promotion costs;
5. Insight from control label team on production, food safety and trends;
6. Exposure to regions that might not have been realistic;
7. Shelf space that might never have been secured;
8. Participation in national events;
9. Flyer space that's devoted to control label might not have been achievable as a branded item;
10. Premium positioning on the shelf for control label.

The disadvantages of producing control label are:
1. The supplier does not have a brand in the market;
2. Retailer has considerable more power over the business;
3. Must comply with audits and retailer defined food safety;
4. There are hidden costs for packaging and events;
5. Some liability for packaging you can not re-use;
6. Some retailers demand exclusivity;
7. Supplier is at the mercy of retailer's sales forecasts;
8. Suppler is impacted by the retailers merchandising, execution and commitment to the item;

9. Volume can be lost due to competitors producing cheaper;
10. A supplier producing for one retailer can have challenges at other retailers, they are perceived to be entrenched across the street.

Suppliers should review the list and determine which attributes are most important in their business. It is a difficult decision to make. Regardless of the company's perspective, suppliers who have an answer for the question before it is asked are most respected.

PLAY YOUR PART

When creating annual sales plans suppliers must consider the efforts the retailers are making to differentiate their offering. Wherever possible support the differences and develop a unique plan for each retailer.

Consider the analogy to children; are you developing a sales plan for the sport focused competitive teenager, the more gentle craft-loving princess or the one with abundant energy and the outgoing personality?

THREE KEY POINTS TO SUPPORT DIFFERENTIATION

1. Develop products and programs to support the positioning of the banners;
2. Treat each retail customer differently;
3. Will you produce control label products in your business?

How can you support differentiation?

CHAPTER 4

SUPPLY CHAIN — THE UNSUNG HEROES

GETTING IT TO THE STORE
IS JUST WHAT THEY DO

Buying, warehousing and distributing products to food stores are some of the most complex and costly tasks for your retail customers to perform. You know how challenging it can be to manage ingredients, production and packaging for the items you produce, now think about buying, warehousing and distributing hundreds of thousands of SKUs. That is what your customer has to do 52 weeks of the year. Keep in mind some of these items are fragile, temperature sensitive, date sensitive and range in size from a packet of spice to 48 rolls of toilet paper.

Retailers call this the "supply chain" and it represents approximately 10% of the retailer's total expenses. For retailers, the supply chain is an expense that is a necessary evil. Getting product purchased and through the system to the store is necessary, but there is no value added to the consumer. Retailers measure supply chain as a percent of sales and cost per case. Every penny below the competition in cost per case is an advantage. This is money that can be reinvested in new stores, pricing initiatives or extra service. Most retailers have three segments in the supply chain: buying or procurement, warehouse and distribution. There are complex systems to operate these functions and manage the large volumes that go through the network.

The efficient execution of these functions can have a significant impact on sales and store conditions. In-stock position is critical for keeping consumers and employees happy. Continued out-of-stocks will drive shoppers to the store across the street faster than many other issues and employees dislike having to explain why items are not available. Service level is measured carefully and people throughout the organization are aware of the level of execution. Most retailers strive for service levels higher than 95% and when this number drops below 90%, consumers will certainly notice it in the stores.

RETAILERS HAVE TO DO IT CHEAPER AND FASTER

There are many variables in delivering a strong service level. Accurate data integrity, good forecasting, concise planning and dependable suppliers are all important factors. Many retailers including Walmart and Loblaw celebrate the suppliers who deliver dependable service level and they also publicize the poor results. In the lobby of Loblaw's head office in Brampton, Ontario there is a large board with the good and the bad. You know where you want to be on that sign.

Every item in the retailer's system has many data points associated with it and one error or omission can prevent an item from flowing through the system. It is critical for suppliers to understand listing forms and provide accurate information.

Product arriving on time and in good condition can be the difference between a successful selling season and a poor one. Food sales can be very time sensitive; stuffing mix does not sell very well on December 26. There are many steps that must be coordinated to have the item set up in the system, priced properly, purchased from the supplier, inventoried in the warehouse, picked for the order and delivered to the store. All of these things must happen and the product must arrive at the store looking just like it did when it was manufactured. Suppliers play an important role in making sure their product is ready for the distribution system.

Finding employees to work in stores and warehouses is becoming more challenging all the time. Keeping existing employees content is also an ongoing challenge. The supply chain segment of the business has a significant impact on both of these initiatives. Automation in the warehouse allows the retailers to focus human resources on the tasks where they are really needed. Assembling solid pallets that arrive in good condition with the right items has a big impact on employee satisfaction at store level as well. Product ready for sale is infinitely more desirable at the store and ensures store employees can focus on their tasks as opposed to incurring shrink or fixing someone else's mistake.

Supply chain is a huge area of focus for retailers and much of it happens behind the scenes. One of the biggest strengths of Walmart is this part of their business. It is very good at buying and very efficient getting the products through its system to the stores in a timely manner. Most of our traditional retailers are trying to catch up to Walmart in this area. **If Walmart can get a case of product through its system for 80 cents less than the competition, this is a huge advantage.** This affords Walmart the opportunity to reinvest this money in lower prices or new stores.

Buying, warehousing and distribution are the three segments of supply chain for retailers. I cannot emphasize enough that suppliers need to understand that buying is part of supply chain, not merchandising. Suppliers work with the merchandisers or category managers to get the product listed, on the shelf and advertised. The buyer is in a different part of the business where the actual purchase order is initiated. Obviously they work together, but as retailers move to more central procurement, buying decisions are made from forecasting systems as opposed to actual category knowledge and experience. Many departments, especially produce, have unique seasonal trends and it is very complex with the origins of product changing throughout the year. You do not negotiate with buyers, but you can be a tremendous resource to them. Buying too much, too little or at the wrong time can have a huge impact on the stores and suppliers.

ROCKS TO THE ROCK?

Centralized procurement has had its growing pains. When I was at Loblaw, centralized procurement was implemented in Lawn & Garden.

One of the first years we had a call from a Dominion store in Newfoundland. They had opened the truck with the first order of garden décor for the season. As they were setting up the garden centre, they were amused to see that we had sent them many cases of plastic rocks as garden décor items. There are many things they do need in Newfoundland, but plastic rocks are not one of them!

The garden centre manager was quite amusing on the phone. In her distinctly unique accent she proceeded to tell me, "Don't be wasting yer money sendin' any more of them rocks. We got more than enough of the real ones." It is wrong to manage a business from a spreadsheet and it is important to take a step back and consider details. Producing plastic rocks in China and shipping them on a boat, a train and a truck to Newfoundland really does not make much sense. We had some fine-tuning to do before people in central procurement understood the needs in different regions.

SYSTEMS RUN SUPPLY CHAIN

After the product is purchased it usually goes in a warehouse. Some product goes direct to the store if it is bulky, high volume for an ad or date sensitive. Warehouses are very costly to operate and the cost of the inventory gets a lot of focus within supply chain. As we say, "product does not sell from the warehouse" so it needs to move through quickly to the stores. Today's warehouses are extremely automated and it is common for the people picking orders to have no idea where it will be going or what is going there. They are being directed by the system and product is really just a number. They usually do not question it, they just fill the order. I have seen huge quantities of very low selling items go to a store because of an error in the system. Data integrity is critical here as there is no time or money to invest in double-checking the work.

There are many reasons retailers push the product through the warehouse. One is this is the first line of defense for quality problems. Product is inspected upon arrival and the retailer will make the decision as to whether they will take possession of it. This is difficult for some suppliers to accept; they long for the days when they could deliver product direct to the store. It is true that quality control will be done much more effectively at a small number of warehouses as opposed to the back door of the store. Product specifications and standards are becoming more sophisticated and the tools required can be used at the warehouse. Suppliers must respect the quality control process and implement processes within their own organizations to ensure specs are met or exceeded. A poor reputation for product rejections will lead to a bad relationship with the retailer.

If you do have product rejected, follow up on the situation. Did you and your customer have the same interpretation of the standard and was it applied fairly? If your product does not meet the spec then treat this as an opportunity. Determine where your organization fell down and communicate any improvements to the retailer. You can turn a negative into a positive with your reaction. It is counterproductive to fight the rejections if your product does not meet the product spec.

RETAILERS MUST CONTINUE TO IMPROVE

There is continuous change in this part of the business. The warehouse used to be a large building constructed to hold a lot of product and they were located all over the place. This has evolved to very few, automated and sophisticated buildings that are designed to get the product in and out as fast as possible. Orders are now assembled to arrive in store with items from the same aisle on the same pallet to make it more efficient. Think about coordinating that when you have stores with different configurations.

It is interesting to get some insight into the retailer's warehouse. Sobeys has invested considerably in supply chain. Investments have been made in technology to reduce the labour required and improve the accuracy of orders being delivered to the store. Sobeys website has an interesting video (which can be found in the Resources section) that provides a virtual tour of their warehouse in Vaughan, Ontario.

Once product flows into the warehouse and gets picked for an order, the final job for supply chain is to get the product to the store. We all see the trucks on the road and anyone in business today knows that putting a product on a truck is costly. The cost continues to increase and at certain times of the year it is difficult to find the space you need as the volume of available trucks goes up and down. Retailers all experiment with their own fleet of trucks, contracting it out or a hybrid. Aside from being a great traveling billboard, trucks are a huge cost and require a lot of coordination.

TRUCKING COSTS BIG BUCKS

Retailers are always working to figure out how to get more on a truck and send the truck to the store fewer times per week. It is always a tug of war between supply chain and retail. In departments such as produce, we would like to get a truck every day at the store to ensure we have the freshest product. This drives sales and reduces shrink. The supply chain part of the business would prefer to add six pallets of potatoes and cabbage to the back of the truck to fill the space and only deliver to the store four times per week. They would say "we might sell more if we have more and we would probably order it the next day anyway."

Delivering on trucking efficiencies represents millions of dollars to Walmart. In their simple yet effective business model they strive to "deliver more and drive less." This is a quote directly from the Walmart website:

> "Walmart U.S. Logistics is an industry leader in the development and testing of advanced fleet technology as we work toward our goal of doubling our efficiency by 2015. We're already 69% more efficient, compared to our 2005 baseline.

> "Since 2007, the Walmart fleet has delivered 361 million more cases while driving 287 million fewer miles."

These statements imply they are also saving a lot of money. Delivering more cases and driving fewer miles translates into significant savings that can be passed on to the customer or reinvested in more stores or more staff.

Trucking is an often overlooked function. If your retail customer has a back haul program, investigate to determine if it is right for you. There might be changes required in your business such as shipping at night, but in the end you might save and you are more entrenched with them.

The three functions of supply chain; buying, warehousing and distribution all touch every part of the retailer's organization and they impact suppliers. The consumer never sees it but your relationship and efficiency within the supply chain system can be the difference between success and failure. Supply chain is constantly evolving and as a supplier you need to continuously learn about your customer and on what they are focused.

Many retailers have back haul programs where they pick up supplier's products after they deliver to the store. These can be mutually beneficial for reducing costs and delivering sustainability initiatives. It is important to explore every opportunity to become an integral part of the organization. They will not keep your item because you are on the back haul program but they might offer more volume if you are part of the solution.

Reusable plastic containers (RPCs) are being used or investigated by many retailers in perishable departments such as produce. This will affect suppliers, supply chain and retail. There is a lot of coordination to get these containers from the supplier, through the warehouse system, back from stores and cleaned before they return to the supplier to start the process all over again. Change can be a challenge, but if  your customer is going to implement these, it's preferable to learn early and determine how they can work within your organization.

Product traceability is one initiative that continues to evolve and requires more resources to execute. Consumers demand for food safety, government regulations and the retailer's own requirements are forcing suppliers to provide significant information associated with the product as it flows through the supply chain system. Understand the requirements now and in the future and have processes in place to deliver the data.

Some retailers are considering flow systems where the product comes from the supplier in store specific amounts and simply gets cross-docked as opposed to being entered in to inventory. Your customers are continuously trying to learn about the most efficient way to operate a warehouse. This will have an impact on suppliers as product might have to arrive at the warehouse in store specific quantities.

SUPPLIERS MUST EMBRACE SUPPLY CHAIN

As we discussed, your business should be focused on the three major areas: buying, warehousing and distribution. Make sure you develop good relationships with the buyers. Do not discuss pricing or listings with them but help them with seasonality, lead-time, data integrity and ad volumes. They are buying what the system tells them to buy. You have experience and a much more narrow focus. Don't question every order, but when you know something is wrong make sure you offer to help them. They are doing what they do for a reason, so don't assume they do not care. Just work with them to understand your perspective.

Often the position of a buyer is an entry level position. Never assume they understand every item or the department where it's being sold. If the buyer is replaced you might have to go back to the basics. Often it seems that as soon as you get them trained they will get promoted, so accept that and make it part of your business planning in developing good relationships.

Buyers do not have reasons to leave their desks very often so they are one of the few people you can call or email and get a timely response. Do not abuse this but work with them when appropriate. Your sales team should be reviewing the orders from your retail customers. If the order does not look correct follow up and provide some facts that might help the buyer make a better decision. You cannot question every order but if there appears to be a significant issue it's better for the supplier and retailer to address it in advance. The holiday buying periods and key seasonal fluctuations should receive extra focus. This is where you can provide real value to your customer.

As a supplier you need to understand your customer's supply chain system. This is an integral part of their business and it can have a significant impact on your results. Every retailer has a unique approach to supply chain. They are all trying to purchase products and get them to the store in the most efficient manner, however, there are many different solutions to this challenge. Store network, geography, store format all influence the design of the ideal supply chain network. Challenge your employees to articulate what your retail customers are doing and the impact it will have on your business. You should do this at least three times per year.

FOLLOW YOUR ITEM THROUGH THE ENTIRE VALUE CHAIN TO ENSURE IT DELIVERS THE EXPERIENCE TO CONSUMERS AS YOU HAD INTENDED.

Learn as much as you can about the warehouse. Any time they offer a tour take advantage of it. Do not walk around and stare up at the racking. Look at what is happening and how they are doing it.

Is your label on the box easy to read?

Do your cases stack properly on the pallet?

What can you learn from other suppliers?

Many of your customers use other retailers who are world leaders as models. Determine what these companies do for warehousing, chances are it might be coming your way.

When the retailer has supplier meetings to share their direction, never question their sanity in front of the crowd. I have been at produce meetings where a person supplying one or two commodities wants to have a debate about warehouse systems. Understand what the retailer is trying to do and how it will affect your business. If the impact is negative (which it can be) find the right venue to have a productive conversation.

YOU ARE PART OF THE SOLUTION

Your customers are very focused on service level and suppliers need to be too. Customer specific service level should be an area of focus for producers and processors. Share the information with your customers and resolve any issues creating service level challenges. Many times the retailer's process or execution can have a negative impact on a supplier's ability to service the customer. Have open and honest discussions to resolve the issues, they want the product on time as much as you want to get it to them on time. Have these discussions with the right people. You might need to request a meeting with merchandising and supply chain to ensure the solution works for all involved. In these big organizations they often have no idea what is happening in different divisions.

Service level issues do arise and despite all of the best efforts you might not be able to supply your customer what they need, when they need it. Communicate as far in advance as possible when you are going to have a service level issue. A missed order is one of the biggest frustrations for your retail customers. If you can give them advanced warning you will be better in the long term. They might even cancel the order but you are more likely to get another order if you allow them to react in advance and rectify the situation before it hurts the store and the consumer.

EDUCATE RETAILERS ON YOUR ORGANIZATION INCLUDING THE PRIORITIES AND CHALLENGES YOU FACE. DO THIS SUCCINCTLY AND RESPECT THEIR KNOWLEDGE OF THE INDUSTRY.

Often the supply chain part of the retailer's business will be more willing to work with suppliers than merchandising. The key negotiation happens between the supplier and the merchandisers, you do not have to negotiate with supply chain. You can offer to be part of the solution and work collaboratively on projects. Offer suggestions and ideas you have been exposed to in other markets. Seek opportunities to learn if you have the opportunity to travel to other countries.

There is a lot more to the retailer than just the store.

THREE KEY POINTS TO WORK WITH SUPPLY CHAIN

1   Focus on all three areas of buying, warehouse and distribution;
2   Make sure your item flows efficiently and effectively through the entire supply chain system;
3   Work with supply chain on initiatives and projects.

How can you work with the supply chain?

_____

_____

_____

_____

_____

_____

CHAPTER 5

FOOD SAFETY IS NON-NEGOTIABLE

FOOD SAFETY SHOULD KEEP US UP AT NIGHT

If you were to ask the management in food retailers, "what keeps you up at night?" Food safety would be the top of the list for many. This is one issue that continues to plague our industry. We all want to satisfy the consumer and deliver food that is safe for them and their families. Food recalls happen every week. Food safety issues are never positive and they undermine a lot of good work done by a lot of people.

When there is a food recall, it is the retailer's store who gets mentioned as often or more than the offending supplier. For branded items, specific SKUs are included but retail stores also have to be mentioned in the recall and in the media. Retailers have purchased the product in good faith but now are associated with the food safety issue. For perishable products that are not branded, retailers are associated even more as the headline will read "Ground beef from store ABC."

Retailers take their role of providing safe food very seriously. Any time there is a food safety issue it can undermine the relationship retailers have with consumers. Everyone knows it is tough enough to generate loyal customers and a lot of good work can be unraveled with one issue. If consumers lose their confidence in stores to purchase and provide safe food they will find another place to shop.

Product recalls cost everyone a lot of money. As an example, we will use a recall in the meat department. There is no doubt this will have a devastating impact on the supplier. They have to shut down production and focus an enormous amount of energy and resources to figure out what happened. They must ensure that the problem is resolved and that they are meeting regulatory requirements. Once solutions are in place, they have to begin the process of building confidence again in their brand with customers and consumers.

One factor that can get lost is the cost to retailers. The first task is to remove any product from the store shelf, then remove it from the distribution system. This is very costly as the retailer has already paid to distribute it to the store, put the product on the shelf and then pay people to reverse all of these tasks. Obviously the priority is to keep the food safe for customers but do not lose sight of what these recalls cost in labour and product. Recalls also force retailers to put resources in to tasks that do not add anything positive to the shopping experience.

Almost every food safety issue can be traced back to an incorrect process or a process that was not followed properly. An example of this would be cleaning a saw in a meat production facility. An incorrect process would be cutting different varieties before cleaning whereas a process not being followed would be to not clean, despite a standard operating procedure that says to clean between varieties. This is frustrating for retailers who purchase product in good faith. There is no doubt these breakdowns are not done maliciously, however, it is the responsibility of producers or processors to maintain safe practices. When issues arise it puts significant strain on the relationship between the retailer and the supplier.

Retailers have their own food safety practices to implement and maintain. Most food stores include some form of food preparation and they have a responsibility to ensure their own processes are in place and followed. For this reason your retail customers are knowledgeable and have very specific requirements.

The retailer's expectation is that suppliers will take food safety as seriously as they do. This has to be one area where retailers and suppliers work together effectively. Knowledge in this area has increased significantly in recent years and there is no excuse for not building internal capabilities for a quick response. There are many resources available to assist in the development and implementations of food safety programs.

NON-NEGOTIABLE REQUIREMENTS

There are a number of food safety requirements for retailers. The primary determination for standards is the department where you will be selling your products. It is imperative that suppliers are well informed about the expectations of the customer. All retailers have people assigned to food safety compliance and they all require certification from third party audits. Investigate the specific requirements you will be expected to meet or exceed. It is important when you are selling product in more than one department to review the expectations specific to that particular department.

There are several food safety programs available to suppliers:
1   Global Food Safety Initiative (GFSI);
2   British Retail Consortium (BRC);
3   CanadaGAP;
4   On-Farm Food Safety Recognition Program.

These food safety programs were established 10 to 15 years ago to provide consistent third party audits that were functional and dependable for retailers and food processors. Prior to 2000, there were many different audits being done and no consistent application of safe food production practices. The following is a summary of the most common food safety programs in place.

GLOBAL FOOD SAFETY INITIATIVE (GFSI)

GFSI was created in 2000 to replace retail driven audits and to address several high profile food recalls. Consumers were concerned about the safety of food production and industry's response was to support a nonprofit foundation. The purpose was to reduce duplication of audits and to harmonize the application of food safety standards. GFSI is a widely accepted accreditation for food safety and third party audits are performed across Canada.

BRITISH RETAIL CONSORTIUM (BRC)

Originally the BRC Food Technical Standard was created in 1998 to evaluate retailers' private label manufacturers. Until this time, each retailer had their own standards and audit process. BRC Global Standards was an initiative started in the United Kingdom that has evolved in to a global standard for food manufacturing processes. Many retailers in different countries have adopted the BRC standards and audit process. A number of retailers will only accept private label products manufactured in a BRC approved facility with an up to date audit.

CANADAGAP

CanadaGAP (Good Agricultural Practices) is a program designed specifically in Canada for companies that produce, pack and store fruits and vegetables. Most Canadian retailers will require CanadaGAP certification for produce vendors. CanadaGAP is recognized by the GFSI. Third party audits are conducted and certification is provided with a score to successful applicants.

ON-FARM FOOD SAFETY RECOGNITION PROGRAM

The Canadian On-Farm Food Safety Recognition Program was developed by Canadian food producers, the Canadian Food Inspection Agency and Agriculture and Agri-Food Canada. This program was developed to provide producers with a framework for implementation of safe food practices. Many producers use the detailed commodity specific information available to develop operating practices and procedures.

Retailers each have their own definition of food safety requirements and it's incumbent upon suppliers to be familiar with them. One of the challenges with these requirements is they are not readily available. There are some generalities that can be reviewed but retailers perceive this to be proprietary information and do not post it on line.

In general, if you are going to produce a private label product you must be certified by GFSI and/or BRC and be audited annually. This is industry standard. For branded grocery products, retailers do not have any specific requirements. They recommend that you are audited by a third party annually and comply with all government regulations for food handling, food production and food processing. It is not possible for them to police all of the different manufacturers and they leave that for CFIA and other government regulators.

In perishable departments, the guidelines are more evident and within the last few years, retailers have become more demanding in terms of compliance. Larger food retailers require produce suppliers to be CanadaGAP certified and audited annually. In meat departments, larger retailers will only purchase product from federally inspected facilities because the distribution networks cross provincial borders. These facilities are certified by CFIA.

Implementing hard and fast regulations for food safety is a challenge for retailers. They would all agree that it is the right thing to do and the best assurance they are providing safe food for their customers. There are two significant challenges:

1. The consumer is demanding more local food to be made available;
2. Food produced outside the borders of Canada.

Smaller suppliers are not always compliant with food safety regulations and they do not produce in volumes that make food safety affordable. It is very costly to implement and monitor all the processes required to be accredited by GFSI, BRC or CanadaGAP. The retailer is faced with a dilemma; satisfy consumers who want locally produced food or satisfy consumers who demand all the assurances possible for safe food. There is also an unfair playing field created for producers who do invest in infrastructure to follow the described processes and complete the reporting. These producers incur costs the others do not.

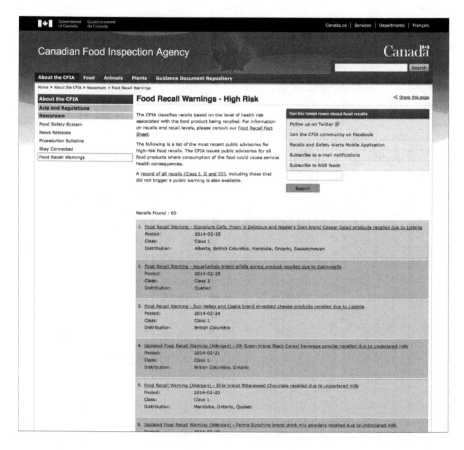

Policing and compliance with processors in other countries is very difficult and very expensive. Consumers are demanding global foods, however, they also demand safe food. Again, there is an unfair playing field for Canadian producers forced to comply with food safety regulations competing against products from all over the world with different (lower) costs of production.

These two dilemmas will be increasingly debated as the food industry moves forward. It is interesting to note that the two largest food safety recalls in the Canadian food industry were from large domestic producers. The Maple Leaf sliced meat recall from 2008 and the XL Foods recall from 2012 both had a significant impact on the health of consumers and cost the industry millions of dollars. Both of these companies would have had relatively sophisticated food safety infrastructure prior to the recalls. Food producers and processors should be aware a food safety issue can happen to any company at any time.

SUPPLIER'S ROLE IN FOOD SAFETY

It is imperative to understand the regulations your customers impose for food safety. You must also assess the level of risk within your own business. Consumer confidence that a product is safe for their family, friends and community is critical for long-term success in the market place.

FOOD SAFETY SHOULD ALWAYS BE TOP OF MIND.

When working with your retail customers there is nothing worse than saying, "no one has died yet." Producers and processors who do not take food safety seriously in their business will not survive in today's environment. This might have worked in the past but it will not work any more.

Food safety must be a priority in your business and people must be accountable for execution and results. These employees should report to the leaders in the business to ensure they are not influenced by people focused on sales or production efficiencies. These employees should develop relationships with food safety personnel at the retailers. This is an area where collaboration is possible and effective for both retailers and suppliers. Good working relationships with these people will pay dividends if there ever is an issue. There are many opportunities such as industry events or one on one conversations for your food safety employees to meet their retailing counterparts.

Challenge your employees to stay current with a retailer's expectations for food safety. Your food safety and sales people should work together on this. They both need to understand what the customer is looking for and both need to have the assurance that your products meet or exceed requirements.

The food safety people in your organization should forge relationships with the food safety people who work with your customer. They are both focused on similar goals and the more your customer understands about your commitment the better. If you have an incident, major or minor, you will be in a much better position to resolve the issue.

Your food safety and sales people should update the management team at least four times during the year on this topic. Their update should include what retailers are demanding, how your company is doing and also where retailers are going. Food safety requirements add costs and if you do not prepare properly they will add even more costs and have a serious impact on your reputation.

If you do have an issue make sure you are up front and honest. Many in the food industry are familiar with the listeria outbreak in Maple Leaf sliced meats. This was a devastating incident with loss of life or severe illness affecting people across Canada. One of the positives to come out of a very terrible situation was that the people working at the highest level of Maple Leaf worked to resolve the situation with retailers. There were regular conference calls where the Maple Leaf CEO Michael McCain was present and a driving force to work through the details and he appeared in media to reassure consumers as well as the industry. Food safety issues are terrible but when they are managed properly with customers, consumers and the media they do not have to be devastating. Maple Leaf foods did take a financial hit as a result of this, however, the company did rebound from it. Maple Leaf sliced meats are sold across Canada today and consumer confidence has returned to a level where the items compete for leadership in the category.

There have been other examples where the processor has not accepted responsibility and consumers were left watching a battle between industry and government played out in the media (which you cannot control). This does not build confidence with retailers or consumers. Issues need to be corrected with an immediate need for ownership and accountability for all involved.

Food safety should keep us up at night because it is a very serious issue. Our ability to provide safe food is a partnership and the only successful partnerships are ones where all involved buy in to the process and execute it flawlessly. Everyone in the value chain must respect each other's roles with the ultimate goal to provide safe food.

THREE KEY POINTS TO KEEP FOOD SAFETY FRONT AND CENTRE

1. Understand the regulations and ensure you meet or exceed your retail customer's expectations;
2. Make food safety a priority in your business;
3. If you have an issue be up front and honest.

What food safety issues do you need to focus on?

_____

_____

_____

_____

_____

CHAPTER 6

HEALTH & WELLNESS SELLS PRODUCTS

CONSUMERS ARE CHANGING FASTER THAN WE THINK

Overall, the population is getting older and that brings new opportunities for people producing and selling food. Consumers are much more aware of the food they choose to buy for themselves and their family. Access to more information and increased focus on health issues have provided us with a much more astute consumer seeking out products with better health attributes. We all want to take that drink from the fountain of youth and live a longer, healthier life.

Health and wellness is also a priority for retailers because there is a good halo effect. Consumers who perceive retailers as trying to help them by providing healthier alternatives develop a more entrenched relationship with the store. On average, these consumers are more profitable for retailers. Margins on healthier items are higher and there are fewer retailers discounting these items.

DIET RELATED DISEASE CHANGES
WHAT GOES IN THE SHOPPING CART

Consumers are becoming much more aware that diet can have a significant influence on their health. Many diseases can be directly linked to a person's diet. One of the most obvious examples is obesity. The Public Health Agency of Canada released a report entitled "Obesity in Canada" where they stated that approximately one in four Canadian adults are obese, according to height and weight data from 2007 to 2009. Another staggering conclusion was that obesity rates had roughly doubled for males and females between 1981 and 2007 to 2009. Obviously diet is not the only influence on obesity but it is a significant contributor.

Heart disease and stroke are two of the top causes of death in Canada. Diet, especially consumption of sodium has a major influence on high blood pressure (hypertension). According to the Heart & Stroke Foundation of Canada, "on average adult Canadians consume about 3,400mg (roughly 1.5 teaspoons) of sodium per day. This is significantly above the level recommended as the upper tolerable limit for health, which is 2,300mg per day (approximately 1 teaspoon)." On the Heart & Stroke Foundation website, the #1 recommendation is for Canadians to eat less processed food.

Diabetes is another chronic disease that is directly related to diet. The Canadian Diabetes Association estimates that 3 million Canadians have type I or type II diabetes and a staggering 6 million are living with pre-diabetes. The famous Mayo Clinic lists five tips for prevention of diabetes:

1. Get more physical activity;
2. Get plenty of fibre;
3. Go for whole grains;
4. Lose extra weight;
5. Skip fad diets and make healthier choices.

Three of their tips are directly related to diet. Consumers are being educated that diet does have a direct impact on health. It is important for producers and processors of food to understand the guidance and direction being provided to consumers.

As producers and sellers of food we have an opportunity to influence the consumer. There is a growing proportion of the population who will reward the retailer with their patronage if they offer items with a focus on nutrition and merchandise a balanced offering.

CONSUMERS ARE CHANGING THE WAY THEY SHOP

Stand in the aisle and watch how many people pick up a product and turn it around to find the nutrition facts. There might be a requirement soon to make the aisles wider for those people who spend five minutes in the canned tomato section looking for the product with the lowest sodium level.

Nutrition facts tables have only been mandatory since 2005, with a grace period until the end of 2007 for compliance. In a relatively short period of time, consumers have become educated and now seek out this information. Regulations are very specific for manufacturers regarding the execution of nutrition facts tables. It is the responsibility of manufacturers to understand and execute the regulations. These can be found in the CFIA's *Guide to Food Labeling and Advertising* located on the website. This is one area where retailers expect manufacturers to execute flawlessly and there is no excuse for items not in compliance.

Many buying decisions are being made after reviewing nutrition facts and ingredients. Consumers are much more aware of the contents of the food they buy and the focus on health and wellness continues to evolve. We started counting calories and many shoppers were preoccupied with calorie counts. In the 1990's the focus shifted to carbohydrates. Dr Atkin's book *Dr Atkins' New Diet Revolution* and other diets encouraged consumers to drastically reduce their intake of carbs. This reduced sales in departments like the bakery and on items such as the potato. Shopping habits changed very quickly and people simply eliminated entire categories from their shopping cart.

BAKERY GETS DECIMATED

It is incredible how something like the Atkins Diet hits the food industry.

When this program was the rage and consumers were more concerned about carbs than measles, the bakery took a beating. I can remember being in the ad meeting, where each department is allotted a specific amount of space. This space is determined by generating sales and traffic. During this fad, the bakery was reduced to a minor role. They couldn't sell hot gooey cinnamon buns, even if they were less than half price.

The fad did eventually wane and the industry responded with more whole grains and smaller packages. One great thing about the food industry is that the consumer's vote at the cash register is felt very quickly. It is being felt again as consumers explore gluten-free as a lifestyle.

We also had the focus on eliminating trans fats from ingredients. These manufactured fats were having a negative overall impact and food processors were forced to eliminate them.

In the last 10 years we have experienced more focus on reducing sodium in our diet. Food processors have been working to reduce sodium levels in products and in many categories "reduced sodium" products are available. Where there are two offerings, the consumer will decide. The two listings will be reduced to one as shelf space is at a premium. More than likely, the reduced sodium item will just become the item available.

The next wave of focus for health and wellness is refined sugar. There is more information all the time about the impact of refined sugar on the body. Food producers are looking for alternatives to refined sugar such as stevia, an alternative to products containing chemical sweeteners such as Aspartame and Sucralose. This could have an impact on product costing and shelf life. Many shoppers are willing to make the investment to purchase products that are better for their body.

There is a significant amount in the media related to health and wellness. There are many examples of very successful television shows devoted to health and wellness. A product endorsement from one of these celebrities can be the engine to propel a product to incredible exposure and sales. All of this mass media has an influence over what people are looking for in stores.

THE KALE CRAZE

Consumers can change their buying habits very quickly. It is so critical for retailers and suppliers to stay on top of trends. Recently we experienced exponential growth in kale. This product has been on an incredible growth curve since it was labeled a super food and included on many top 10 lists for healthy food.

When I worked in the store, kale was in the produce department but we used more to decorate the seafood department than they sold in produce. Now the growth is reaching 200% to 300% year over year with no slow down in sight. Producers are scrambling to grow enough to meet demand. Consumers are inventing new ways to eat – and drink – this tough, bitter vegetable to ensure they get the health benefits they crave.

The Internet is another source of information for the consumer. There are entire websites devoted to food and products you should put in your body, and those you shouldn't. Food producers and processors must monitor advice being provided to consumers. These trends take time to develop and it is often a significant opportunity for suppliers and retailers to offer an item that has received this type of coverage.

RETAILER'S COMMITMENT TO BEING HEALTHY

Overall, the retailer's commitment to health and wellness is dictated by the consumer. If they support initiatives and buy products then health and wellness will continue to get more focus. Each retailer has invested a different level of resources to health and wellness.

Retailer's commitment to health and wellness is directly related to the economy. If consumers are feeling confidant that their job is secure and they have some discretionary income, then health and wellness will see more growth. When the economy is not healthy and consumers are very concerned about expenditures, they will gravitate to less expensive alternatives that are not as healthy. The reality is products that are good for the body are more expensive to produce, distribute and maintain at store level. Many require refrigeration and they have a shorter shelf life. Retailers are in business to drive traffic in to their stores and satisfy the needs of their customers. They will change their focus to where their customer is going.

No doubt that items with a health and wellness focus are good sales opportunities. Retailers are looking for these items to drive sales and profit. Often this can be a line extension, which will deliver greater overall sales.

STAY ON TOP OF TRENDS. THESE OPPORTUNITIES DELIVER INCREMENTAL SALES. PROFIT AND POSITION YOUR ITEMS DIFFERENTLY IN THE MARKET.

Many retailers have launched healthy alternatives within their private label program and they are making significant investments in store to deliver a better shopping experience for health conscious consumers. Retailers only make these investments if there is a payback at the cash register. With new products being introduced, on shelf programs to identify healthier items and in store dietitians, it is obvious consumers are responding.

LOBLAW'S COMMITMENT TO HEALTH AND WELLNESS

Loblaw has four ongoing initiatives to entice health conscious consumers to visit Loblaw's stores:

1. Natural Value Department;
2. More than 400 Blue Menu items that are a subset of the President's Choice program;
3. They have implemented the Guiding Stars program on shelf in Ontario;
4. Community rooms offer support from dietitians and healthy eating cooking classes.

Many Loblaw banners include a Natural Value Department. This is approximately 10,000 square feet devoted to items that deliver better health benefits, certified organic products or items targeted at a specific health conscious consumer such as vegan, vegetarian or Genetically Modified free. The items in this department are managed by a separate group of category managers in grocery merchandising.

Often the store employee is very knowledgeable in this department as they have a personal interest in healthy eating. The items do not sell as fast as regular grocery and the distribution is different as well. Many are direct store delivery (DSD).

Loblaw's commitment to healthy eating started in 1991 with the introduction of the Too Good to be True line of products. These items were designed to emphasize great tasting options that could also be healthy. In 2005, the line was rebranded under the Blue Menu label. These items are found through out Loblaw stores and they are supported each year with the Healthy Eating Insiders Report. This four week event is supported by a catalogue of new and existing items, POS and significant off shelf merchandising. The primary goal is to bring people in to the store and sell products, however, it's also a significant commitment to healthy eating.

Loblaw develops Blue Menu items in house. These products are tested by dietitians prior to being approved as a Blue Menu item. When a product is approved for the PC Blue Menu line, it must meet at least one of the following nutritional criteria:

1. more omega-3s;
2. more fibre;
3. less calories;
4. less fat;
5. soy protein or less sodium.

Loblaw considers these to be the important pillars of good nutrition.

In 2012, Loblaw tested an in store, on shelf program called Guiding Stars. The program is designed to take the guesswork out of choosing nutritious foods. A simple rating of one to three stars on items throughout the store provides guidance for consumers. Shelf labels on each SKU identify the number of stars. In 2013 the company made the commitment to launch the program across all conventional stores in Ontario. This is a significant investment in signage and labour to support the program.

The Guiding Stars web site describes the program as:
"An impartial, patented food rating system that rates food based on nutrient density using a scientific algorithm. Foods are rated based on a balance of credits and debits. Foods are credited for vitamins, minerals, dietary fibre, whole grains and omega-3 fatty acids, and debited for saturated fats, trans fats, added sodium and added sugar. Rated foods are marked with easy to follow tags indicating 1, 2 or 3 stars."

This program is designed to make healthy eating easier for everyone. Loblaw must be experiencing some payback at the cash register for the company to roll this out to more stores. Existing items were rated by Guiding Stars and there is a process to review new listings. There is no fee for suppliers to participate in the program.

Years ago, Loblaw and many other retailers started to add community rooms to store layouts. This was a space that could be used for nutrition classes, cooking schools, children's birthday parties and other community events. Consumers are interested in nutrition and stores are responding with class-

es conducted by nutritionists who work at the store. This is a significant commitment of resources and floor space. There must be a pay back of traffic and/or increased sales for it to continue with new stores being built.

WALMART'S COMMITMENT TO HEALTH AND WELLNESS

In 2011 Walmart addressed the issue of Health and Wellness with their commitment to Make healthier food a reality for all. This initiative included five key elements:

1. Reformulating thousands of everyday packaged food items by 2015;
2. Making healthier choices more affordable;
3. Developing strong criteria for a simple front of package seal;
4. Providing solutions to address food deserts by building stores in underserved communities;
5. Increasing charitable support for nutrition programs.

The progress on these initiatives was updated by Lisa Sutherland from Walmart's Healthy Food Team in November 2012. They were launched in the U.S. division of Walmart but they filter though the international division as well.

"Walmart has removed 1.3 million pounds of sodium from more that 500 foods across three categories."

"We helped shoppers save $1.1 billion on produce in 2011 and are on track to meet this goal again in 2012."

"Walmart opened 53 stores in the last year serving rural and urban areas in food deserts, bringing our total to 275."

"The Walmart foundation has donated more than $15 million to nutrition education programs in the U.S."

As part of their commitment to health and wellness, Walmart launched their Great for You food labelling initiative in February 2012. After reviewing over 4,000 private label foods and beverages, it determined that 32% qualified for the Great for You label. This included produce and lean meats. Labels started to appear in stores in September 2012. The program will continue to roll out as more labels are changed.

SOBEYS AND JAMIE OLIVER

Sobeys have invested in celebrity chef Jamie Oliver to deliver their message of healthy eating. New products and cooking ideas are reinforced in stores and on their website. Focus is on education and making healthy eating a

part of consumer's lifestyle. Shoppers are encouraged to eat at home and cook with natural ingredients.

My purpose for including the different company initiatives is not to rate them or pass judgment. It is to illustrate the commitment some retailers are making to these types of initiatives. Regardless of their intentions, they are making significant investments.

HEALTH SELLS

Health and wellness is a significant sales opportunity for suppliers. Retailers are interested in these items to satisfy the needs of the consumer. Often a line extension building on a current success will be effective. Producers and processors should be reviewing their items to understand where they fit in terms of health and wellness. Your customers are looking for the products. They might not tell you that but they are!

Off shelf display space is more available for items that reinforce a retailer's position on health and wellness. These are great opportunities to drive sales and awareness. End cap or floor displays can increase sales by more than 100% as we have trained shoppers to look for deals and exciting items in these locations throughout stores.

Many weekly ads have space devoted to healthy alternatives. In the past, these items would not have met the criteria to get in to the ad. Sales would not have been high enough. As retailers work to improve their image in this area, they have created theme ads to support healthier options. Similar to the incremental merchandising, these are terrific opportunities to drive sales and increase awareness.

If private label products are part of your strategy, this is an even bigger opportunity. Every one of the major retailers has created a sub brand within their private label offering to address health and wellness. Check out the shelf to understand if they are satisfying the need in the categories where you have capabilities.

Suppliers should be spending time to review ingredient information to ensure it's in line with where the consumer is going. Trans fat was the issue in the 90's, sodium was the issue in the last 10 years and refined sugar is the next focus. Are there opportunities to remove these ingredients and deliver a superior product?

Adding ingredients with health benefits is another opportunity. It seems as though a new super berry is discovered every few years. Most recently it was the acai berry. Do your products have the capability to deliver or include some of these super foods?

Functional foods are another segment of products where there is consumer and retailer interest. These products are developed by providing different inputs to deliver better nutritional qualities. The best example of a functional food is the omega-3 egg. Chickens are fed flax seed as part of their diet. The egg that is produced contains omega-3, which is a fatty acid. This is a good fat humans do not get enough of in our diet. Omega-3 eggs in our market command a 25% premium on the shelf.

Take advantage of these trends as they materialize. Retailers are famous for taking great items and destroying them. When the consumer responds to an item, the utility of the item changes for the retailer. The product shifts from something that increased sales and profits to an item that will drive traffic. This is the retailer's opportunity to discount the retail and reduce the profits to get traffic in the store. If the consumer continues to shift purchasing patterns, the items that drive people in to the stores will be healthy alternatives.

THREE KEY POINTS TO SELL MORE HEALTH & WELLNESS PRODUCTS

1. Retailers are looking for more items to support their Health & Wellness initiatives;
2. Understand Health & Wellness trends to ensure you are delivering products that resonate with consumers;
3. Focus on your unique selling proposition in Health & Wellness with your customer, the retailer, and the consumer.

What Health & Wellness opportunities can you bring to the retailers?

_____

_____

_____

_____

_____

_____

CHAPTER 7

GLOBAL FOODS ARE ON FIRE

WHO THOUGHT WE COULD SELL THESE ITEMS?

The face and tastes of our consumer have been quickly changing. This has a significant impact on items that people are putting in their shopping cart. It is imperative that producers and processors explore trends in immigration to understand what items need to be produced in the next 10 years. Items that were popular and growing five years ago will not be the items of choice in 10 years. Change in production and processing take time and resources. These must be managed carefully to satisfy consumer demand but also to ensure items are affordable for the producer and or processor.

Population growth in Canada is only happening through immigration and the country of origin for new residents is very different than it was in the past. Historically, immigration to North America was from Europe. This has evolved to be dominated by immigration from Asia. This large, diverse continent has many cultures, widely differing tastes for food and economic standing. Immigration is also regional, when people from one country or culture start to settle in one area they form a community. There are examples of this in many North American cities where specific populations dominate neighbourhoods or communities. It is very important for producers and processors to understand the trends in their respective markets. Matching the products to the consumers is critical.

In Canada, we have seen immigration levels of approximately 250,000 people per year, consistent annually since 2008. This level of population growth is significantly higher than the population growth in the rest of the citizens. There are two other sources of new consumers coming to Canada; temporary foreign workers and foreign students. The following table (source: Statistics Canada) illustrates the number of people within each segment for 2012.

Permanent Residents	257,515
Temporary foreign workers	338,189
Temporary foreign students	265,377
Total	861,081

Consumers who come in to the country are bringing their tastes, demand for items and cooking methods with them. There is a distinct advantage for producers, processors and retailers who understand these new opportunities. Exposure to these new tastes, items and cooking methods is also having an impact on consumers who were born in Canada. They are being educated in a diverse array of new meal ideas and they are experimenting along with restaurants that cater to both audiences. These existing consumers are also a significant opportunity for growing sales.

If you see opportunities to expand your sales with selling these items to the traditional consumer, keep in mind education is an opportunity. They might have been exposed to a new taste or dish in a restaurant but without the recipe, instructions and guidance your item might fail. The new consumers understand the items and cooking methods, while the traditional consumers will benefit from some help.

One interesting phenomenon that will slow the growth rates for items is the one-generation effect. A grain farmer from Southwestern Ontario shared this insight with me, which I thought was very interesting. When people come to Canada they want to maintain traditional food and culture, as that is what they are familiar with. When they get exposed to North American diets and tastes, they change. When the immigrants continue to the second generation, the demand for the items the first generation sought out will decrease significantly. Currently we do not come close to satisfying the demand for these global foods but there will come a time when we will so producers and processors will have to watch these trends carefully.

Changes to item mix are happening throughout the store. Every department is changing and in some cases new departments are being created. In the ready to eat sections of many stores sushi is one of the top selling items. It is a great item for consumers to have prepared in advance and it is very portable. It is also a healthier choice than many of our traditional fried or breaded options.

BRIDGEWATER SUSHI

The popularity of sushi as a home meal replacement item exploded. Who would have thought? Raw fish for a premium in Nova Scotia

When we made the decision to add sushi to our stores we had to decide where to make the investments. Each store cost approximately $20,000 for equipment and renovations so we had to select locations where we would re-coup our investment. The usual urban markets were on the list. One of our specialists recommended putting sushi in Bridgewater N.S. This is a pleasant fishing community on the south shore of N.S. Known more for catching fish and processing than consumers craving raw fish and rice. I said 'no way, they don't understand this stuff, they will try to cook it!'

In the end I was convinced to go with this store and was I wrong... Sushi out sold the regular seafood department regularly.

OUR CANADIAN CONSUMER IS CHANGING

It is a tremendous learning experience to visit stores that cater to new consumers. If at all possible, visit the store with a person who is knowledgeable about the items and uses for the products. Many items are still imported, therefore, they are an opportunity for producers here. Importing food products from Asia or any continent can be challenging and costly. Locally produced and supplied items will have a great chance, as long as they are comparable to the items from the originating country or region.

Imported foods used to be a 24-foot section within the grocery department. We would cram in any products available from distributors with no real understanding of the consumer or demand for the items. Rarely would they ever meet the criteria for advertising and because they were not listed in the warehouse, the cost was higher and it was difficult to really do much to promote the items. This is all changing. We are starting to see specific sections in traditional stores dedicated to countries or regions.

FIND OPPORTUNITIES WHERE YOU CAN DELIVER VALUE TO RETAILERS BEYOND SALES AND PROFIT. YOU WILL BENEFIT IF YOU PROVIDE EXPERTISE AND SOLUTIONS.

As these categories continue to evolve there are challenges for retailers. The consumer is more knowledgeable than the retailer. Category managers for global food items are becoming much more informed and retailers had to make choices. They either had to take an existing category manager who was educated in the merchandising practices and systems and educate them about the items or they had to find individuals knowledgeable about the items and educate them about merchandising philosophies and systems. This has improved significantly in recent years but it has been a transition. Employees at store level are also not comfortable working with items they do not understand. There is a need for retailers to invest in their employees to help them understand the items and be able to assist consumers.

Many of the items are produced off shore and do not always flow through supply chain systems effectively or efficiently. Retailers have had to implement manual processes to accommodate the items. As consumer demand grows it's more and more important these items be included in the listing base. Sales build in the markets where the immigration is highest. As consumers move within Canada or get exposed to the products in their travels, demand will grow in the smaller markets.

As population continues to change, retailers are eager to build their expertise in this area. In 2009, Loblaw Companies purchased the T&T chain of supermarkets. T&T was an independent retailer originating in British Columbia. The stores cater to the East Asian consumer and sell a diverse selection of items that are not available in traditional food stores. The purchase of T&T illustrates the traditional retailer's appetite for learning this segment of the market. Loblaw Companies had many other priorities at the time, which included a declining share price in the face of stiff competition from Walmart super centre. The leadership in the business felt it was critical to benefit from the expertise within T&T and to ensure these consumers were still spending their grocery dollars with Loblaw.

New consumers to the market have different buying patterns than traditional consumers. Learn the specific characteristics of your target market. There are some generalities that can be made. Fresh items form a larger part of the diet and shopping is more frequent than our traditional consumers. It is also critical to understand what factors will influence the purchase. Consumers from different ethnic backgrounds have different priorities and criteria for selecting an item.

NEW ITEMS BRING NEW OPPORTUNITIES FOR SUPPLIERS

There is a significant opportunity for producers and processors who want to invest time and resources to develop and supply items to meet the needs of the ethnic consumer and those who relish new products. Vineland Research and Innovation Centre in Vineland Station, Ontario completed some very interesting research to assist producers of primary crops. The opportunity for three items was quantified for producers. Through online research, they were able to determine the market opportunity and potential revenue for some ethnic vegetables. The following table illustrates the amount of product required for three items that would have been difficult to find in traditional food stores 10 years ago.

	ONTARIO DEMAND	POTENTIAL REVENUE	ACRES REQUIRED
Okra	24,900,000 lbs	$ 49,700,000	1,400 to 2,600 acres
Yard long beans	23,700,000 lbs	$ 59,000,000	10,500 acres
Asian long purple eggplant	21,400,000	$ 33,400,000	N/A

The report which can be found on their website, also notes that sales estimates could be underestimated because in 2012, consumers were unsatisfied with the quality. If product was closer to what they are looking for sales could be even higher. These are just three examples of items that are increasingly produced in Canada to meet the demand of a changing consumer.

Suppliers who are knowledgeable about global foods bring value to retailers. They are trying to catch up to the consumer so any information is important. Suppliers who want to produce these items need to develop internal expertise. Consumers are knowledgeable and retailers are developing knowledge. If expertise is not in house, producers and processors need to

go outside to find it. There are definitely sales opportunities but they need to be produced authentically. The consumption patterns of consumers in different parts of the world are very interesting. According to *Watt's Executive Guide to World Poultry Trends 2011*, the average Canadian person will consume 175 eggs per year where as the average person in China will consume 300 eggs annually. With China providing the largest number of new Canadians each year, this is an opportunity for the egg industry. The eggs that are popular in China are different than the eggs produced in Canada. Consumption is spread across different poultry and some of the eggs are preserved. Presently the eggs available at the T&T store in Ottawa are from both domestic and imported sources. A Canadian producer could explore this opportunity and produce different eggs using the traditional methods.

Developing expertise to produce items is one option for suppliers; importing product is another. Consumer demand is there and consumers seek out traditional items produced in the original country. There are other items that just will not grow in our climate or we do not have the raw materials available for production. It's also important to understand labeling requirements for importing. These issues will continue to evolve as local producers put pressure on government to monitor offshore items for food safety and undeclared ingredients.

These items are getting more and more exposure in store and in weekly ads. This will drive execution at retail and more volume. Suppliers who produce or process these items should be ready for the fluctuations of ad volume and be ready with inventory.

The item is not the only change. Consumers looking for these global foods shop differently. Suppliers must learn how they shop and implement packaging and display options to appeal to these consumers.

GLOBAL FOODS IN BEDFORD NOVA SCOTIA

While shopping in our local Loblaw store I was surprised to see a large display of T&T brand items.

I was more surprised to see the display at the front of the store. Valuable real estate devoted to low selling items, in my mind. I have been in the food industry for 25 years and I did not recognize some of the items, such as brown lumps on a plastic tray from Korea and very dry, pale crackers from Japan. As I was questioning the sanity of the merchandising plan, a woman approached from the produce department.

She already had a beautiful pink dragon fruit in her basket. She selected two items from the display and kept shopping. If you produced these items you got the sale, if you produced something else you probably lost a sale. This was in fact a good use of this valuable real estate and I needed to learn more about a new category.

There is no doubt the listing base in grocery stores will continue to evolve as consumers in the store change. Retailers are scrambling to catch up and there are many opportunities for suppliers. As the market gets more crowded with supply options for retailers, there will be more pressure on costing. Producers and processors who can capitalize during the growth period will benefit. Conduct research to understand the size of the opportunity and stay ahead of a changing market place.

THREE KEY POINTS TO SELL
MORE GLOBAL FOOD PRODUCTS

1. Understand the specific needs in your marketplace; be open to suggestions and monitor new offerings as they are changing quickly;

2. Share your expertise with the retailers, they are craving it;

3. Explore options to produce locally or import.

How can you incorporate global foods into your product mix?

_____

_____

_____

_____

CHAPTER 8

FOOD SOLUTIONS ARE MORE POPULAR THAN EVER

EATING IN CANADA IS CHANGING

Consumers are demanding more items that have reduced preparation time and in some cases they will buy the items 100% prepared or ready to eat. Our society seems to be busier than ever, with less time to prepare meals. Food retailers have had to respond to these demands. Most stores now include a prepared meal section at the front of the store and items throughout other departments are designed to satisfy the time-starved consumer. It is imperative for producers and processors to understand the investment in shelf space being devoted to these items.

Today's consumer has a lot of choice and your customers view any meal prepared with products purchased outside their store as a missed sale. In previous generations, most meals were consumed in the home. Meals eaten outside the home have increased as our lifestyles have changed. According to Statistics Canada, annual household expenditures for food were approximately $7,800 in 2011, of which 27% was spent in restaurants.

It's very easy to drive down a busy street and be bombarded by restaurants or fast food with convenient drive-thrus. They will do all the work and you have the pleasure of eating right in your car. This is all competition for your customers; they have had to respond to ensure sales do not erode further to this very aggressive competition.

Eating outside the home is only one influence on the consumer's meal planning process. Two people working in households have also created challenges for meal preparation. It's difficult to arrive home at 6pm and spend the next hour preparing a meal if you have young children. By the time the baked potato is cooked, it's time for the children to be going to bed. Without significant pre-planning, these families are in need of food items and appliances such as microwave ovens that reduce preparation time.

Another change in our Western society is the mindset that we should run from one organized event to another. Evenings are filled with soccer games, dance classes and many other activities for everyone in the household. It is difficult to prepare a traditional meal between the time work stops and activities start.

While there is significantly more information available to consumers today on food preparation — glossy magazines, cooking shows and the Internet — the irony is not everyone cooks. There are many consumers who do not have the knowledge to prepare meals the way previous generations did. They rely on prepared products in the food stores and have no desire to invest the time in a roast chicken or making a pie from scratch. These shoppers are willing to pay a premium to save time and many are not willing to sacrifice taste.

Our food stores were originally built to satisfy traditional meal preparation and consumers who ate most of their meals at home. The stores and products available have evolved significantly in recent years. Traditionally, consumers in food stores were looking for three meals per day and they would take the time to prepare these meals. Snacking, skipping meals, faster prep time, eating outside the home and eating on the run all have changed the grocery order at the checkout. A prepared tray of cut vegetables and dip will satisfy the hunger and reduce the food required at traditional meal times. There are some who believe many people now consume four meals per day. These are different meals than traditional breakfast, lunch and supper that our food stores were designed to satisfy.

Items that appeal to these new eating occasions are growing in popularity. A cup with yogurt, fresh fruit and granola is the equivalent of a one-stop shop for some consumers. This is an example of a food solution that might displace a dairy item such as butter, which is a more traditional ingredient. Butter will not be eliminated but the linear feet will be decreased to make room for the new item. In the past, stores might have listed three SKUs of butter, now they only have room for the top two. The dairy section does not get any bigger so assortment will change. All of these changes have an impact on the listing base throughout stores.

Food solutions are evolving quickly. In the past, convenience was the only pre requisite, now consumers want convenience, health and wellness and perhaps a food from the other side of the world: challenging tasks for food producers.

Our shopper is much more educated about reading labels and aware of ingredients and nutrition facts. Prepared foods are notorious for high sodium and they have the potential to contain many different forms of sugar. People are sending the message they will not trade off health for convenience and they are rewarding items that deliver both attributes.

Global tastes, new ingredients and demand for foods from different cultures are also driving sales of food solutions. There has been exponential growth in items with these attributes. Consumers are more willing to try these meals if some or all of the preparation work is done for them.

FOOD SOLUTIONS ARE WINNING
There are a number of reasons that retailers are evolving their mix to in-

clude more food solutions. The most obvious reason is to satisfy consumer demand. The options for the consumer are directly across the street, therefore food retailers have had to adapt quickly.

Differentiation from other food retailers is another objective in the prepared food departments. These are great opportunities to put a unique offering in place and generate some consumer loyalty. A well-executed home meal replacement department can be the difference between two competitors. When the consumer needs a tasty BBQ chicken and side dishes they will stop in the store that delivers the best and most consistent offering. These departments are very challenging for retailers. The labour, food safety and shrink can all be a challenge for stores and employees. In most stores these departments are at the front and when they are good they really do bring customers in, when they are bad they are a very expensive project. Whole Foods Market does a great job with prepared foods. The selection is broad and their merchandising entices the consumer to buy. I would go to Whole Foods before I would go to many restaurants.

Margins on prepared foods and food solutions are all usually higher. As margins decline in certain departments with increased competition stores are striving to find higher margin options. Prepared food margins are very high to absorb high labour and shrink. In a properly operated department, contribution should be much better than most other departments. In a good prepared foods department the contribution should be more than 20%. Margins are higher on the food solution items in other departments because the items are newer and the retails have not been forced down. The consumer is willing to pay a premium for convenience.

The final reason retailers are devoting more space to food solutions is to increase private label penetration. Private label is a form of loyalty in that a consumer who really likes the store brand will continue to patronize the store. Many food solutions are delivered to the market as private label. Often it is smaller manufacturers who have some specialized equipment or process but do not have the marketing expertise or resources to deliver a branded offering.

All of these factors have influenced selection in food stores. There are examples of food solutions in every department and almost every category. A food solution does not have to be an entire meal. It is critical for producers and processors to plan for the future and stay ahead of trends.

Entire categories shift and demand for yesterday's item is very low. It is also important to understand category structure within your retail customers. Each category will command a certain number of linear feet within the store. This is determined by sales, profit and the store configuration. If the category manager you work with has a lot of new food solutions available, it is probable some other items will lose shelf space or be de-listed. There is only so much linear footage available and if an item is a food solution that satisfies our changing consumer, it will get the space. The number three brand in a declining category of three offerings will be displaced. It is fascinating to explore the store and watch as the categories evolve.

SINGLE CUP COFFEE TAKES OVER!

One significant shift implemented recently is in the coffee category. This category used to be divided between whole beans, ground and instant. The shelf space would be approximately 40% whole bean, 40% ground and 20% instant.

The huge growth of the single serve coffee makers forced retailers to reline the entire category. New single serve products command up to 50% of the shelf space with the

more traditional items reduced proportionally. This is great if you are sell-
ing the new products and have evolved into a more profitable item. This
can be devastating if you are only selling whole beans.

The new generation of single serve coffee makers is an example of a food
solution. The consumer gets the identical quality every time, there is no
mess and the array of choice is incredible. You can offer one guest a cap-
puccino from Starbucks and another guest a Tim Horton's coffee without
leaving your kitchen. Simple, quick and satisfies many different tastes, at
a premium price per cup.

The prepared dip category in the deli department is another example of food solutions generating sales and profit. Items that were never even available in North American supermarkets such as tzatziki and hummus are now household words. My five year old daughter knows what they are. I did not know what these products were until I was in my twenties. These items are prepared with natural ingredients and they appeal to consumers for many reasons. They are relatively good for you, they bring global items to your own kitchen and they only require opening the plastic container. Every year these items take more shelf space from other deli SKUs.

Seafood departments contain a number of prepared food items and food solutions. Many consumers want to eat seafood but they do not know how to prepare it, do not have access to fresh ingredients and they are not fond of handling the raw product.

WISH I HAD THOUGHT OF THIS ONE!

One of the best examples I have seen for a food solution is in the seafood
department. I still remember the first day I saw the product, before it
was available in the grocery stores. Doug Park formed Cedar Bay Grill-
ing Company with the intention to introduce some salmon items to the
market. We met to discuss the items and when he pulled his frozen cedar
planked salmon from a small cooler bag my first thought was "why didn't
I think of that?" The idea was so simple, so effective and it had great po-

tential. He had figured out how to pre-soak the cedar plank, add the sea-soning to the fresh fish and flash freeze the entire product.

The result was a healthy product that had all of the prep work done. Pre-soaking a cedar plank is not always convenient and salmon has a very good reputation for health. The product was versatile in that it could be prepared on the BBQ or in the oven. After several years of hard work the product is being distributed in grocery stores and food service in many North American markets and Europe. Cedar Bay Grilling planked salm-on is an example of a prepared food that earned space in today's food store.

Produce is one department where the commodity items dominate and value added offerings are a recent addition. Visit the refrigerated juice section in your local food retailer to see more examples of food solutions. Many stores have 20 different SKUs of prepared smoothies and fruit/vegetable drinks. These are more examples of taking work away from the consumer and earning better margins. If you calculate the actual fruit that would be needed to create these items there is a definite premium being paid. Consumers pay for the convenience of opening the bottle instead of peeling fruit and putting it in a blender. These items are promoted as healthy alternatives and many include

information about how many servings of fruits or vegetables they deliver.

Similar to fruits and vegetables, meat is driven by commodities. A number of meat companies started to introduce raw items with seasoning, such as poultry, but now you can find easy carve turkeys and even cooked meats. However meat items have more opportunity to improve nutrition as many include significant amounts of sodium.

Grocery has a lot of private label and tastes from around the world. In the late 80's and 90's Loblaw created a category with the President's Choice Memories Sauce line up. The first was Memories of Szechuan peanut sauce and the line grew to exceed 20 SKUs. These items introduced the consumer to many different tastes and added meals to household menus. Lettuce wraps with peanut sauce are very popular with everyone in our house. We never ate meals like that when I was growing up.

In most aisles of the grocery department you'll find food solutions with frozen food having the highest penetration. Frozen food offers a dizzying array of food solutions. From breaded fish to skillet dinners there are choices for everyone. Categories for adults such as shrimp fettuccini or snacks for kids such as pizza pockets are available. An opportunity for food producers is to watch items introduced in frozen and figure out how to deliver the item fresh. Consumers will purchase the frozen offering, however, if there's a fresh alternative it's preferred.

Retailers are making significant investments to provide food solutions to their consumers. We have discussed all of the changes evident within the listing base but resources are being committed elsewhere too. Retailers are working very hard to make their store and their websites a destination for food solutions. These are opportunities for food producers and processors as well.

Many stores now include rooms for cooking classes where shoppers can be educated about food solutions. Every possible theme is included in the schedule, one more example of the consumers driving change in the offering. Any space in a store is valuable so if retailers are building these rooms, staffing them and investing other resources there must be a return.

Websites of retailers are full of meal solutions and similar to the cooking classes, this comes at a cost. Consumers can search for recipes, learn about ingredients, cooking methods and products. There are interactive blogs and idea exchanges that engage the consumer of today. Producers and processors should explore these websites to understand what retailers are saying to their customers.

Cooking programs and websites are opportunities for suppliers to increase their value to retailers. Many food production companies have their own resources and these can be made available to retailers. The relationship you have with your customers does not always have to be limited to item and price. You are further entrenched with your customer if you can provide information, recipes and resources to help them deliver their own food solutions.

You and your experts can develop a different type of relationship with your customer. This does not replace the negotiation between a supplier and the merchandisers but it does bring value that your competition might not be willing or able to deliver.

SUPPLIERS NEED TO BE TRENDY

Food solutions and prepared foods are a sales opportunity in today's retail environment. Suppliers should explore the possibilities and be ready for continued change in the listing base of retailers. Items will be in demand in every department. Focus on healthy ingredients and processes that maintain health benefits. Introduce tastes and ingredients from local cuisine or the other side of the world. It is very important to visit stores and look for trends within categories.

Cooking with new ingredients or methods can be challenging. Prepared meals will satisfy less adventurous cooks. Availability of ingredients has evolved as the world becomes a smaller place. Consumers are becoming more aware of ingredients such as acai berries in prepared smoothies or piri piri seasoning in prepared meats. Food can be similar to fashion in that there are trends that will change rapidly. Producers and processors must be aware of what is happening in high-end restaurants and the leading edge communities. These establishments set trends that eventually find their way to grocery stores.

The science and technology of food production is also evolving very quickly. These new opportunities for improving quality, shelf life and perhaps even health and wellness are commanding shelf space within stores.

New categories have been created to satisfy the growing demand for food solutions. There are opportunities to target adults with such time savers as shrimp fettuccini skillet dinners in frozen foods or children with Lunch Mates in meat departments.

Prepared foods and food solutions receive ad space that is disproportionate to their sales. Retailers are willing to accept lower sales on these ad items to showcase the product and reinforce differentiation. Take advantage of these ads if you have appropriate items. Often they are built on themes such as meal occasions, foods of the world or time saving ideas. Propose all the potential themes where your items fit. Category managers might not always consider your item as being an opportunity in several of these ads.

Margin generated by food solutions items is important. Work with your customers to ensure prices offer value for consumers but try to stay away from deep discounts. Retailers are very good at eroding the perceived value of items with deep discounts. They bring people in once but the value of the item is decreased. Retailers set the retail but wherever possible focus on inside ad opportunities where price is not as critical. Do not try to set retails but wherever possible avoid the temptation to offer deep discounts.

The opportunity for food solutions will continue to grow for retailers and suppliers. Consumers are putting more and more of their grocery dollars in to these items, as nutrition, taste and convenience evolve. It is also critical for the long-term health of retailers to keep people shopping in stores and out of restaurants.

THREE KEY POINTS TO SELL MORE FOOD SOLUTIONS

1. Monitor trends for items, ingredients, cooking styles, immigration, production and other influences;
2. Put resources into developing products that have a direct benefit to the consumer and are not presently available e.g. Cedar planked salmon;
3. Explore existing items to update ingredients, technology and packaging to make aspects more enticing to retailers and consumers.

What food solutions can your business offer to the marketplace?

_____

_____

_____

_____

_____

_____

CHAPTER 9

CORPORATE SOCIAL RESPONSIBILITY – DO THE RIGHT THING

There are four basic areas of CSR:

1. Sustainability;
2. Sourcing;
3. Employees;
4. Community.

Suppliers should be focusing their efforts around these four areas. It is also important for a company's CSR program to reflect the company itself, not only what customers are focused on. To be effective it must be true to the values of the organization.

WHY RETAILERS WANT TO DO THE RIGHT THING

The pioneers of corporate social responsibility (CSR) did it because the leaders saw it as the right thing to do. Now companies have no choice. They have to include sustainability, ethical sourcing, workplace issues and the community in their business priorities. Consumers demand it.

There is so much more awareness around these issues now than 15 years ago. Issues such as the environment and ethical sourcing are in the news regularly. Companies are penalized if they do not strive for a leadership position.

Walmart, the world's largest retailer, has paid more than $100 million since 2010 for violating the Clean Water Act in California. On two separate occasions, Walmart pleaded guilty to illegally handling and disposing of hazardous materials.

Loblaw was the lead story in print and television news in April 2013, following the collapse of a clothing factory in Bangladesh that killed more than 1,000 workers. Loblaw did not own the factory, however, some of the Joe Fresh clothes were manufactured there and by association, the company was perceived to be responsible.

Our retail environment is very competitive and there are too many stores. Consumers have choice and many will not support stores where they see gaps in the company's corporate social responsibility plan. Today's marketplace is full of transparency and there is nowhere to hide. With the different applications on the Internet such as YouTube and Facebook, stories spread very quickly and consumers have the ability to share their opinion and in some cases, deliver feedback directly to retailers.

In December 2012, Loblaw was the focus of a YouTube video claiming that they had mistreated a supplier. One of the supplier's co-founders uploaded a video that was a personal plea to Loblaw's executive chairman, Galen Weston. In six months more than 231,000 people viewed the video. The story was covered in every major newspaper as well. There is a Facebook group called "Do the right thing Loblaw" that people can join. Retailers must be very careful how they operate. Bad news travels very fast.

Major food retailers are big businesses and they have a significant impact on our environment. With more focus on global warming and energy consumption, retailers are front and centre. Plastic bags going to landfills, trucks driving thousands of kilometers and stores using huge amounts of energy for lights and freezers are all very visible detriments on the environment.

Environmental groups and customers have been vocal about retailer impacts on the environment. Retailers have been forced to respond with plans and investments to reduce or offset some of these issues.

Another reason for the retailer's commitment to sustainability is that they have been forced into it. Walmart took a leadership position, which forced their competitors to address the issue. There was no way other Canadian retailers could ignore the environment when Walmart was making claims about energy use and reducing or eliminating garbage. Walmart even organized a Green Summit meeting in 2010 and invited the competition! That was a bold move in the competitive world of retail. Participants included representation from every major consumer packaged goods company and other retailers. Canadian Tire, Loblaw, Home Depot and others sent employees to the Walmart event. David Suzuki was a keynote speaker and the event was covered by all major media. The race to leadership in the sustainability arena was on.

CSR can have a positive influence on the bottom line. Reducing garbage at retail stores and offices reduces the expense of garbage removal. Decreased energy use has a direct impact on the expense line. These are all positives that can be reinvested in to lower prices, more service or profit for shareholders. During the 2010 conference, David Cheesewright, President and CEO of Walmart Canada at the time, proclaimed that the company's sustainability initiatives would save $140 million. In an interview in the March edition of *Canadian Grocer*, Sobeys claim savings of $500,000 in their N.S. stores. According to Keith Ross of Sobeys, it accomplished this by cutting energy use.

The final reason retailers all include CSR in their business priorities is that they just want to do the right thing. No doubt these are big businesses but most of them do have a conscience and people working within deserve credit for spearheading these initiatives. Many are passionate about the environment, their fellow employee, employees in foreign countries and the community. Working on CSR with your retail customers can be a rewarding experience and an opportunity to improve the relationship you have with your customer.

SEE CSR AS AN OPPORTUNITY!

CSR programs include vast opportunities for suppliers. Retailers are saving money with these programs such as waste diversion; garbage is a big cost. Are there opportunities to reduce your costs and do the right thing for the environment?

What are you doing about your trucks and energy use in your plant or overall operations? Have you looked at alternative energy and reduced packaging? If you haven't already, initiate your own sustainability audit to be proactive and engage your employees.

Many retailers have CSR objectives tied to fundraising for children's charities or employee initiatives. You should explore these opportunities to improve the relationships you have with your customer. Often these are tied to social events where you can sponsor a charity run or host a community event. You will not negotiate at CSR events but you should continue to nurture the relationship you have with retailers.

Remember to talk to your customers about what you are doing to support these initiatives. You want your customer to see you supporting the positive direction in which they are heading. Your relationship will be stronger if you volunteer to participate as opposed to having your participation mandated.

JUST WHAT ARE THEY DOING?

It is very important that suppliers understand retailers' CSR programs and where the supplier fits. It is interesting to explore CSR initiatives. They are a great example of how retailers are trying to accomplish a similar goal with their own unique approach. Walmart has a simple four step commitment.

Loblaw has a long, complicated list of goals and objectives, Sobeys is in the middle with defined goals but nothing revolutionary, then for companies such as Whole Foods it is a way of life.

Different approaches are a great reflection on each company's approach to business. This is a great lesson for suppliers about how you should approach each company differently. CSR is a true reflection of the heart and soul of the business. Your relationship will be much more effective if you work with them in the manner they choose to approach CSR.

The true measurement for CSR is not a percent reduction in one or more categories, it is in the store, with the customer and the employees. If the program created by a particular retailer is effective, this is where you should see it reflected, not on a piece of paper.

CSR programs are well defined on the retailers' websites and every supplier should re-visit these regularly to watch for updates and changes. I will explore each of the different programs in this chapter.

WALMART

1. Environment
   a. Be supplied by 100% renewable energy
      i. Reduce greenhouse gases at our existing stores by 20% by December 31, 2012
   b. Create zero waste
      i. Reduce in-store food waste by 10% by December 2015
      ii. Reduce plastic shopping bag waste in Walmart's international stores by 50% by December 31, 2013
      iii. Reduce packaging by 5% by December 31, 2013
   c. Sell products that sustain people and the environment
      i. Purchase all wild caught fresh and frozen fish from fisheries certified to the Marine Stewardship Council standard or equivalent by December 31, 2013

    ii. Work with aquaculture certification organizations to certify that our farmed fish suppliers adhere to Best Aquaculture Practices by December 31, 2013

    iii. Source all tuna from International Seafood Sustainability Foundation members by December 31, 2013

    iv. Committed to sourcing 100% of fresh produce from Canadian sources when in season and available

    v. Increase our organic assortment to 5% of produce sales by December 31, 2013

    vi. Require sustainability sourced palm oil an all private label products by December 31, 2015

    vii. Eliminate 20 million metric tonnes of greenhouse gas emissions from Walmart's global supply chain by December 31, 2015

2. Ethical sourcing

  a. Drive change through high standards and factory audits

    i. Complete audits for 100% of factories supplying direct-import, private label and non branded merchandise for all retail markets by January 31, 2012

    ii. 95% of direct import factories receive one of two highest ratings in audit for environmental and social practices by January 31, 2012

    iii. Ensure 86% of our domestic suppliers' private label and non branded factories in the U.S., U.K. and Canada receive one of two highest ratings in audit for environmental and social practices by January 31, 2012

  b. Partner with our suppliers to identify and implement solutions for improving factory conditions

    i. Enroll approximately 100 suppliers in the Supplier Development Program annually

    ii. Improve worker dormitory standards and canteen conditions globally in supplier's factories

    iii. Enhance chemical and machine safety in supplier factories through training, improved hazard protection safeguards and strengthened ethical sourcing program requirements

  c. Provide women working in supplier factories with the life, health, communications, technical and leadership skills to increase social opportunities

    i. Establish training programs for 60,000 women in 150 factories in India, Bangladesh, Central America and China over the next 5 years

  d. Proactively advocate for policies and practices that promote dignity and respect for all workers in Walmart's supply chain

    i. Meet and exceed all requirements in the California Transparency in Supply Chain Act and expand our efforts to make a significant contribution to global anti trafficking and anti slavery efforts

3. Community Investment

  a. 72 construction/remodel jobs planned for 2012

  b. Generate more than 14,000 store, trade and construction jobs

  c. Expand multi cultural product assortment in Store of the Community program

4. People

  a. Strengthen our current engagement framework, improve management and millennial associate engagement by examining and addressing their unique engagement concerns

  b. Implement new practices and training to strengthen diversity and inclusion in our home office and leadership teams

  c. Strengthen core leadership development and enhance merchandising and operations capability

  d. Continue to create thousands of new employment opportunities as we expand into new markets across Canada

SOBEYS

It is interesting to note that Sobeys lists collaborators beside several of their initiatives. They are working with organizations outside of their company to realize some of their objectives.

1. Direct operations
   a. Reduce greenhouse gas emissions by 15% by December 31, 2013
      i. Reduce carbon footprint in stores, distribution centres and fleet
      ii. Reduce electricity consumption in stores and distribution centres
   b. Reduce refrigerant leaks in stores
   c. Reduce waste to landfill by 30% by December 31, 2013
      i. 48% of all waste was diverted from landfills in 2012
      ii. Recycling and composting reduced waste by 55,000 metric tonnes

2. Supply Chain
   a. By 2013 stop selling any species with significant issues unless an improvement plan is in place
   b. A 5% reduction in private label packaging by 2013
      i. Focus on reducing environmental footprint of packaging with more recycled materials, materials that are commonly recycled and packaging weight reductions
   c. 50% reduction in plastic bags distributed to customers by 2013

LOBLAW

Loblaw has an exhaustive list of initiatives related to CSR. It is Canada's largest food retailer so it does touch many different areas.

1. Respect the environment
   a. Waste reduction
      i. 82% waste diversion at distribution centres
      ii. 80% waste diversion from store support centres

      iii. Reduce waste from corporate stores by an additional 5% from 2013 levels

      iv. 20 additional corporate stores to divert organics

      v. Initiate pilot programs in 1 distribution centre and 1 corporate store to achieve 100% diversion from landfill

b. Reduce food waste

      i. Partner with food banks to launch a retail food program in 100 corporate stores.

c. Packaging reduction

      i. Implement paper sourcing commitment as it pertains to packaging

      ii. 50% reduction in non-recyclable packaging from control label products by December 2013

      iii. 5% packaging reduction on control brand products by year end 2015

d. Energy reduction

      i. Reduce total energy consumption by 3% per square foot in existing corporate stores

      ii. Complete solar panel projects in 40 corporate stores in Ontario

      iii. Install a transcritical refrigeration system that uses carbon dioxide as the sole refrigerant in 1 corporate store

      iv. Complete lighting retrofits in 70 corporate stores

e. Fuel reduction and fleet efficiency

      i. Replace 75% of transport fleet with new trucks that comply with U.S. EPA emission standards by year end 2015

      ii. 20% increase in rail use

      iii. 5% increase in backhaul trips

      iv. 5% reduction in driver idle time

      v. Add 10 non diesel burning reefer trailers to our fleet

      vi. Introduce four 60 foot trailers to our fleet

      vii. Install 10 additional lift-a dock systems in our trailers

    f. Water footprint

       i. Conduct a water footprint assessment of our operations

2. Source with integrity

    a. Local

       i. Source 30% of produce sold in Loblaw stores from local Canadian growers

       ii. Source up to 40% of the produce sold in Loblaw stores from local Canadian growers during the peak growing season

    b. Animal welfare

       i. Fresh pork sold in our stores will be sourced from suppliers who have made the transition to loose housing environments by year end 2022

       ii. Introduce a new President's Choice free-run omega egg product

    c. Paper procurement

       i. Implement a sustainable paper procurement commitment for the business

    d. Sustainable seafood

       i. Source 100% of seafood sold in our stores from sustainable sources by year end 2013

       ii. Obtain chain of custody certification for our distribution centres and more than 600 of our stores enabling the sale of both MSC and ASC certified products in our seafood counters

       iii. Participate in the Global Sustainable Seafood Initiative discussions on seafood sustainability and eco-labelling

       iv. Continue to drive consumer awareness of sustainable seafood and be open and transparent about our progress and our policies

    e. Palm oil

       i. Source palm oil contained in all control brand products from sustainable sources by year end 2015

f. Product safety and traceability

    i. Expand Loblaw academy to remaining control brand vendors

    ii. Implement quality and safety management systems for non food control brand products

    iii. Implement quality and safety management systems across ethnic control brand products

    iv. Achieve 100% Global Food Safety Initiative certification for all control brand produce growers

    v. Develop a consumer food safety education program in stores

3. Make a positive impact in our community

    a. Health and wellness

        i. Roll out Guiding Stars in all remaining stores in Ontario (excluding No Frills)

        ii. Roll out Guiding Stars in all stores by year end 2015

        iii. Conduct 20,000 patient touch points (i.e.. Risk assessments, vaccinations and medication reviews)

        iv. Conduct 1,000 community education sessions in stores

        v. Designate 200 dietitians nationally to support the "Healthier Home Event"

        vi. All President's Choice brand products to be free of artificial flavours and colours

        vii. Reduce sodium in 200 existing control brand products by an average of 16%

        viii. Develop 300 new control brand processed products that meet our internal guidelines for responsible sodium content

        ix. Develop an action plan to reduce sodium in remaining control brand processed products through to 2016

        x. Enhance colleague corporate wellness program

    b. Community giving

        i. Continue to give to charities and non profit organizations across Canada with a focus on Greening our Communities,

Healthy Active Kids, Feeding Our Neighbours and President's Choice Children's Charity

4. Reflect our nation's diversity
   a. Implement external programs to recruit targeted community groups such as Aboriginals, new Canadians and persons with disabilities by year end 2014
   b. Build a multi-year organization strategy to align with customer and colleague accessibility requirements
   c. 100% increase in diversity champion programs in 2013
   d. Increase the number of women in leadership roles in the organization
   e. Expand the "I speak" program to all corporate stores by year end 2014
   f. Expand our range of authentic multicultural products across our Rooster Brand, T&T and Suraj control brands by 50% by year end 2014

5. Be a Great Place to Work
   a. Colleague engagement
      i. Roll out new colleague recognition program
      ii. 3% increase in colleague understanding of Company shared values
      iii. 2% increase in colleague awareness of corporate social responsibility
   b. Accelerate leadership effectiveness
      i. Increase number of leadership focused training programs available to colleagues
      ii. Expand our manager ready program
      iii. 2% increase in participation of e-learning and instructor led training courses
   c. Health and Safety
      i. 10% reduction in total accidents

METRO

1. Respect the environment
   a. Making responsible choices in every aspect of the business in order to minimize our environmental footprint
      i. Improve sustainable packaging criteria on private label products
      ii. 10% reduction in energy consumption by 2016 using 2010 as our baseline
      iii. Achieve a 25% reduction in waste sent to landfill by 2016 using 2010 as our baseline

2. Delighted customers
   a. Our customer centric approach is at the very foundation of our business and the key element of our corporate responsibility strategy
      i. To continue expanding our Life Smart product line, making it even easier for our customers to make healthier food choices. A series of initiatives that adds to that action, also helping us promote health and nutrition
      ii. To continue implementing Global Food Safety Initiative standards to our produce and our private brand products
      iii. To expand the scope of our Sustainable Fisheries Policy to include our private brand grocery products, while at the same time working with our suppliers for the continuous improvement of sustainable fishing methods
      iv. To further expand our line of Eco-Selection products which are Eco-Logo certified or that offer a strong environmental aspect with respect to the market

3. Strengthened communities
   a. Making a positive contribution to the communities in which we operate and source our merchandise
      i. We will invest in communities more strategically for an

          amount equal to 1% of our average net earnings over the last three years

    ii. We are working to define Metro's significant commitments to promote local procurement

4. Empowered employees

    a. A top priority for Metro is the creation of an ethical, safe and healthy work environment with a dynamic culture of respect, diversity and professional and ethical conduct

        i. Continue to implement initiatives to reduce the number of overall injuries and ensure upgrade activities for our in-store equipment in order to eliminate the risks related to machine safety

        ii. Continue to focus on the prevention and reduction of occupational injuries in our establishments

        iii. Give additional customer service training to store employees through our Customer Promises program

        iv. Continue to roll out our employee survey to better meet their expectations

TARGET

Target's CSR program is based on the company's operations in the U.S. All objectives are based on the U.S. business, however, they are starting to make some commitments in Canada. On the Target Canada website they list some donations to United Way in Toronto and team members volunteering in Mississauga, Ontario. They also make the commitment that their head office and all stores they open in Canada will be certified to Leadership in Energy & Environmental Design (LEED) gold standards.

1. Education

    a. Double education support

        i. Double Target's year end 2009 cumulative support of education with a focus on reading, to $1 billion

    b. Improve more school libraries
        i. Complete 42 more Target School Library Makeovers at in-need schools
    c. Increase reading proficiency
        i. Increase reading support
        ii. Implement literacy pilots
    d. Increase book donations
        i. Donate 2 million books as part of the Target School Library Makeover and Target Books for Schools Award programs
    e. Increase Take Charge of Education (TCOE)
        i. Increase cumulative giving to schools nationwide through Target's signature TCOE program to $425 million

2. Environment
    a. Reduce waste
        i. Reduce the amount of operating waste sent to landfill by 15%
    b. Reduce water use
        i. Reduce water use by 10% per square foot
    c. Reduce greenhouse gases
        i. Reduce scope 1 and scope 2 greenhouse gas emissions by 10% per square foot and 20% per million dollars of retail sales
    d. Increase Energy Star certifications
        i. Earn the Energy Star for at least 75% of U.S. Target buildings
    e. Improve transportation efficiencies
        i. Improve the efficiency of general merchandise transportation inbound to distribution centres by 15% and outbound by 20% and support the adoption of cleaner and more fuel efficient transportation practices

3. Sustainable products
    a. Increase sustainable seafood selection
        i. Ensure that our fresh and frozen seafood selection is 100% sustainable, traceable or in a time-bound improvement process by FYE 2015

b. Improve own brand packaging sustainability

    i. Enhance at least 50 owned-brand packaging designs to be more sustainable

4. Health and Well being

    a. Increase health assessments

        i. Increase the percentage of team members and spouses/domestic partners enrolled in a Target health plan completing a health assessment to 80%

        ii. Increase biometric health screenings

            1. Increase the percentage of team members and spouses/domestic partners enrolled in a Target health plan completing a biometric health screening to 80%

    b. Increase team member health engagement

        i. Increase breast cancer screenings

            1. Increase the percentage of eligible team members and their families enrolled in a Target health plan getting breast cancer screenings to 76%

        ii. Increase cervical cancer screenings

            1. Increase the percentage of eligible team members and their families enrolled in a Target health plan getting cervical cancer screenings to 79%

        iii. Increase colon cancer screenings

            1. Increase the percentage of eligible team members and their families enrolled in a Target health plan getting colon cancer screenings to 63%

        iv. Increase diabetes HbA1c testing compliance

            1. Increase the percentage of eligible team members and their families enrolled in a Target health plan getting diabetes testing to 91%

        v. Increase use of financial tools

            1. Increase the percentage of team members participating

in the Target 401(K) who are using financial tools and resources provided by Target to 30%

5. Volunteerism
   a. Increase volunteer hours
      i. Strengthen local communities and help kids learn, schools teach and parents and caring adults engage by increasing team member volunteer hours to 700,000 annually

COSTCO

It was more difficult to find a definitive CSR plan for Costco. There is nothing on the Canadian website and it was a challenge to find it on the U.S. website. There is a 2012 sustainability report which lists some accomplishments in the areas of energy, waste and carbon footprint. There are no objectives available for the public or reports to assess the company's performance.

With 85 locations in Canada, it will be interesting to see if consumers put more pressure on Costco in Canada. They employ a low cost model, which has been successful for them however there is an expectation from the consumer and employees. This might or might not impact them at the cash register, only the members will decide.

The four areas identified in the 2012 annual report are:
1. Reducing the carbon footprint;
2. Enhancing energy management systems;
3. Expanding packaging design initiatives;
4. Further developing recycling and waste management systems.

The same letter to shareholders refers to the global impact of Costco's supply chain. They reference responsible sourcing for several items and the positive impact through out the chain. The challenge for suppliers is that expectations are not clear.

WHOLE FOODS

Whole Foods has a very compelling CSR position. They communicate more of a philosophy or way of life as opposed to a defined list of measurable objectives. Certainly this business was founded by a group of individuals who were passionate about CSR and this is one of the reasons for the considerable success they have enjoyed. In their Green Mission Report they outline their position on sustainability:

"Our decentralized company structure, in part, explains our initial approach to reporting on our sustainability initiatives. We approach these efforts differently, too. Instead of a Director of Sustainability or an Environmental Committee within the Board of Directors, environmental stewardship is built into individual jobs, teams, stores, and operating regions. Every Team Member has environmental responsibilities such as recycling and responsible energy use; most stores have a "Green Mission" team, and several of our regions devote part-time or full-time positions for Green Mission Specialists to educate Team Members and promote the company's Green Mission goals."

The company does list a set of core values, which are their version of CSR. The list includes the following:
1. Selling the highest quality natural and organic products available;
2. Satisfying and delighting our customers;
3. Supporting team members excellence and happiness;
4. Creating wealth through profits and growth;
5. Caring about our communities and our environment;
6. Creating ongoing win-win partnerships with our suppliers;
7. Promoting the health of our stakeholders through healthy eating education.

There is no doubt some CSR initiatives had to take a back seat during the recession. Companies were focused on survival and some investments had to be postponed to ensure financial stability. Now that the economy has stabilized or at least found a new normal these initiatives will get more focus.

JUST WHAT ARE YOU DOING?

Producers and processors should have their own CSR plan and my recommendation is for the individual who owns this to also own interpreting the retailers program. Often there are opportunities to develop new relationships and collaborate with your customers. Suppliers should understand the retailers' position and their expectations. This can be very broad and

refer to everything from energy use to ingredient sourcing to package design. You must be familiar with what retailers expect.

In Canada there was a foundation set up by the retailers. This was diminished in strength when they lost the participation of all of the major retailers. Some retailers have their own charity or foundation. I recall some suppliers being upset that retailers would implement these. There was a feeling that retailers would mandate the donations and take credit for the gifts. One has to take a step back and remember why they are doing it as opposed to who will get the credit.

My expectation is that some retailers will implement sustainability audits. They will require suppliers to meet specific targets for energy consumption, packaging weight and ingredient sourcing. Now that retailers are starting down this path, the rest will follow. Suppliers should be ready!

CSR CAN BE A SALES DRIVER

There are sales opportunities for suppliers who can develop items that meet criteria for sourcing and development. Many retailers are looking for branded and control label items such as seafood, produce and items from developing countries. If you choose to brand your products remember to tell the story. Your customers and consumers want to know, this can be an important point of differentiation relative to your competition.

One of my favourite questions to ask produce suppliers was "how are you doing with labour?" I would ask the question because it helped me understand a lot about the supplier. The response would give me considerable insight in to how the business was being managed. If the supplier responded that they had no issues, employees would come back year after year even for seasonal jobs, then that was a good indication I was working with a company that treated employees well. If the response was that people were not dependable, not willing to work and it was a disaster, then I would have some doubts. I would ask myself 'why they had so many challenges, was there more to it than a poor work force?' If the response was it was tough to find skilled labour but they were being proactive and participating in off shore labour programs then my estimation was they were doing the best to address a difficult situation. The responses were always a good indication of the overall business. The response would also be an indication of where the company was going with CSR and the treatment of employees. I still believe that a company that invests in the workforce is a better company to work with. A reliable labour pool will produce better products more consistently; two of the best sales drivers there are.

Programs for sustainability, sourcing, employees and community can all have a positive impact on an organization. If your organization is supporting these initiatives they should be reflected in your product. Consumers will respond. This is the type of program that will help you build relationships with consumers. These people are looking for your product for more reasons than just a price.

Retailers depend on suppliers to deliver the best product they can that is safe and on time. Companies that work to treat employees properly and motivate them have a better chance of success. There are many great products that underachieve because they are just a great idea that was not well executed. Retailers put a lot of faith in suppliers, suppliers have a direct affect on a retailer's reputation. You want your customer to have the confidence you will deliver. A well executed CSR program in your own business can be the difference. A company that earns a reputation for doing the right thing will be rewarded by consumers and retailers with more sales.

THREE KEY POINTS TO UNDERSTANDING CSR

1. Understand the unique initiatives from each retailer;
2. Develop a CSR culture within your business;
3. Find common ground with retail customers and work together.

What are examples of CSR within your business that will result in a better reputation and drive more sales?

_____

_____

_____

_____

_____

_____

CHAPTER 10

THRIVING IN THE FOOD INDUSTRY

THRIVING IN THE FOOD INDUSTRY

Operating in the food industry is like preparing a delicious meal. Many ingredients must be assembled to produce the final product. One poor quality ingredient or one missing ingredient will have a significant impact on the ultimate success of the meal.

Remember; if it does not make it in to the shopping cart, it will not stay on the shelf.

The ingredients:
Food safety
Efficient production
Consistency
Points of differentiation
Efficient distribution
Continuity of supply
Customers
Employees who execute

Regulatory compliance

Planning for the future

Consumer acceptance/loyalty

Profit

Sales & marketing

Priority alignment with customers

A MUST FOR A SUCCESSFUL RELATIONSHIP

We have focused on the priorities of retailers in the previous chapters. Now it is imperative to incorporate the customer's priorities in to business planning and the business model of the supplier. Understanding priorities is one thing, incorporating them in to the recipe will get your items in the shopping cart.

It is imperative to have a balanced approach. Food producers and processors must have a business model that will produce products, generate a profit and keep customers happy. One of these factors cannot outweigh the others or the company will not be successful. My intent with this chapter is to focus on the customer part of the equation, it is not to say that production or profits should not be areas of focus.

Success = producing products + profits + satisfied customers

My experience working with different producers and processors is that they are much happier when they are producing a product and a profit. They are passionate about production and profit, understanding the customer and trying to figure out what they want is a chore. Unfortunately this consideration is often left to the end of the process as opposed to being a part of the process. This is a reactionary approach that is ineffective and disruptive.

When priorities of customers are considered up front during business planning, they can be incorporated in to business objectives. This is a proactive approach that's a recipe for positive results.

DOES YOUR BUSINESS NEED A FRONT-END ALIGNMENT?

Many of us have experienced driving a car where the wheels are out of alignment. The car will run and get you to your destination, however, it is not a very enjoyable experience. The ride is not smooth and if you don't get your car in to the shop you will cause long-term damage to your tires. Alignment in business is just the same. If you stay in alignment with your customers you will have a smoother ride and avoid damaging parts of your organization.

PRIORITY ALIGNMENT

Priority alignment is an effective exercise that provides a snapshot of how your priorities relate to your customer's priorities. There are three requirements to complete the exercise:

1. Customer priorities;
2. Your business priorities;
3. Objective assessment of alignment.

CUSTOMER PRIORITIES

The first thing you need is a well defined list of your customer's priorities. This is a great starting point. The people in your organization need to have a clear definition of what's important to your customers. This is not a simple task and it takes some time. Sales and marketing employees should be able to articulate the different priorities for each customer.

You need to have a separate list for each customer. They all have sales as a priority but will define it differently. For example: one retailer might be focused on growing comparable store sales and another is committed to driving traffic in to new stores. If you sell to Loblaw and Walmart, they have different strategies for sales so it's important to capture these discrepancies.

Different priorities should be defined as accurately as possible. To be effective, it's important to understand the details. If you identify one retailer is committing resources to global foods you need to be more specific. To ensure your alignment is effective you need to have a good understanding of their focus in global foods. They could be working on growing sales 15% in the next three years but your business is committed to a project that will not produce material results for four years. You both have the same priority but you will not be recognized for your efforts.

There are a number of sources for finding the business priorities. You can always access the most recent annual report from the retailer's website. Often they will outline business priorities for the upcoming year. Business updates are also provided by the retailer's leaders at conferences throughout the year with their presentations available on company websites. If you're unclear about their position ask them to clarify it. This is a great way to ensure you have clarity and it also illustrates to them that you are trying to incorporate their areas of focus in to your business.

Once you have the priorities, rank them from most important to least important. This should be done for each retailer, from their perspective.

YOUR BUSINESS PRIORITIES
The second thing you need is a well defined list of your business's priorities. These priorities should include the person responsible within the business for each initiative. During the planning process they should act as the advocate or spokesperson for this initiative. Each owner should have all details and rationale behind this business priority.

Some businesses will have unique priorities for different customers, which should be included here.

Once you have the priorities, rank them from most important to least important.

OBJECTIVE ASSESSMENT OF ALIGNMENT
The third thing you need is an objective approach to the exercise. You will have to assess where your business is heading relative to where your customer's business is heading. Some businesses have the ability to do this internally and others will need to find an outside resource to ensure the process is objective. It's critical to be honest and avoid the temptation to defend the

plan. Often we are proud of the work we've done and it's difficult to see that the business does not match up well with your customer's priorities.

Regardless of the approach you choose it's time to evaluate if you are enjoying a smooth ride or in for a trip to the shop for some alignment.

THE PROCESS

The goal of this exercise is to create a visual chart to summarize the relationship between the priorities in the supplier and each retailer. I like to use a simple green, yellow and red system, which I'll detail in the next few pages. Set up a separate page for each customer. You will find blank priority alignment charts at the back of this chapter for your use.

Start by listing the ranked priorities of the retailer on the vertical axis. In Chart 1 these are identified A-F. Start at the bottom (A) with the most important priority and continue up the axis with each different priority. Using the ranked priorities will help you assess where it is worthwhile to make change and where the pay back will be lower. The closer the priority is to the bottom the more important it is to the retailer.

List your business priorities across the horizontal axis. In chart 1 these are identified as 1-5. Start with the most important priority and continue across to the right. The closer the priority is to the left the more important it is to your business.

CHART 1   CUSTOMER: ABC STORES
RETAILER'S PRIORITIES

	1	2	3	4	5
F					
E					
D					
C					
B					
A					

YOUR BUSINESS PRIORITIES

OVERALL ALIGNMENT

The first thing to understand is how the overall priorities line up. If the retailer has sales as the first priority (which many of them do) and sales does not appear until the middle of your priorities, then you need to reflect on this. If you both have sales as the first priority then continue up and across to ensure there is more alignment. You will not be aligned on everything; they have their business to run and you have yours. You should not change everything you are doing but there does need to be some common ground.

It's preferable to see some alignment in overall priorities such as sales, differentiation etc. In the bottom left side of the chart where the most important priorities intersect you should be finding good alignment. If you have different areas of focus in the upper right these are less critical.

In Chart 2 both companies have sales as their most important priority. They each have their own perspective on sales. As you move through the retailer's priorities there are some which can be found in the suppliers and some gaps.

CHART 2 CUSTOMER: ABC STORES

RETAILER'S PRIORITIES

	INCREASE ABSOLUTE SALES 5%	REVIEW PACKAGING FOR RECYCLING	ELIMINATE GLOBAL FOOD ITEMS	INTRODUCE FOOD SAFETY AUDIT	IMPLEMENT NEW PACKING LINE
100% SUPPLIERS GFSI CERT.					
OPEN NEW DISCOUNT BANNER					
REDUCE ENERGY COSTS 20%					
OFFER 250 MORE GLOBAL FOOD ITEMS					
IMPLEMENT NEW MIS SYSTEM					
INCREASE COMP SALES 3.5%					

YOUR BUSINESS PRIORITIES

PRIORITY ALIGNMENT

Once you've had a chance to review the overall alignment, you need to make an objective assessment of how close you are to your customer. This will provide you with a picture of where you should take advantage of opportunities and where you might need to reassess your business priorities.

Take each of your priorities and determine if they are truly in line with the customer's corresponding priority. For example: if you both have sales as a priority, how close are the details. As I noted in the process above, I like to use a simple green, yellow and red system:

GREEN

Green signifies very close alignment. You are both working to a similar goal and this is an area where you should share results and accomplishments with the customer. No change is required in your organization and if you meet your objectives the customer should see this as a win. The areas with green alignment should form an integral part of your plan with this customer.

YELLOW

For a priority to be yellow there is some alignment, however, it is not 100%. With some changes in your organization, this could become green. The questions that must be answered are whether the priority is important enough to the customer to warrant the change and if there will be a payback to you for making the change. If the priority stays yellow it's not detrimental to the long-term relationship with the customer. Yellow alignment will require the most discussion. This is where there will be grey areas. Green is a positive that needs to be promoted and red will definitely require action as it has a negative impact on the relationship.

RED

When you review the corresponding priorities and the organizations are going in opposite directions, they will be red. These priorities require more discussion. The first question is whether this will have a negative impact on the long-term relationship with the customer. If the answer is yes, then you must consider changes to move the priority to yellow. A business must make changes that are contrary to the direction of customers. The most important issue is the affect it will have on the relationship.

In Chart 3 I applied the green, yellow and red assessment to each corresponding priority. There is some alignment but these two businesses are not aligned on everything. We will explore the priority alignment within each section of Chart 3.

GREEN

- The most important priority to each one is sales so there is a green dot to indicate alignment (1). The retailer expressed their sales in terms of comp sales so when the supplier is creating the annual plan it's important to ensure the 5% growth in the business will meet or exceed the retailer's expectation for 3.5% in comparable stores.

CHART 3   CUSTOMER: ABC STORES

RETAILER'S PRIORITIES

	INCREASE ABSOLUTE SALES 5%	REVIEW PACKAGING FOR RECYCLING	ELIMINATE GLOBAL FOOD ITEMS	INTRODUCE FOOD SAFETY AUDIT	IMPLEMENT NEW PACKING LINE
100% SUPPLIERS GFSI CERT.				2	
OPEN NEW DISCOUNT BANNER					
REDUCE ENERGY COSTS 20%					3
OFFER 250 MORE GLOBAL FOOD ITEMS			4		
IMPLEMENT NEW MIS SYSTEM					
INCREASE COMP SALES 3.5%	1				

YOUR BUSINESS PRIORITIES

YELLOW

- There are two yellow dots, which indicates some alignment but not 100%. In the area of food safety the retailer is expecting GFSI certification and the supplier is going to start with audits (2). It might be necessary to change the priority of the supplier to get GFSI certification. Sales could be lost if this is not addressed.

- The other yellow dot is in two different priorities (3). The retailer is working on sustainability and the supplier is looking to improve efficiency with a new packing line. The reason for the yellow dot is that the new line will reduce energy costs by 25%. This is an opportunity to share the priority with the retailer and get some credit for reducing energy costs.

RED

- In our example we have one priority with a red dot (4). The retailer wants to increase the offering in global foods and the supplier is going to stop producing global food items. If the decision is being made at the supplier because raw materials are not available, that is something that must be discussed with the customer. Explain the reason; despite the fact you understand they want to expand you have no option but to cease production. If the supplier is stopping production because they do not see this as an area for growth and focus at the retailer, then this should be reconsidered.

- We see some areas where there is no alignment. The retailer is implementing a new MIS system and also introducing a discount banner. Both of these could be opportunities for the supplier. Perhaps items targeted at discount stores could be included in this year's plan? Extra resources should be allocated to work with the retailer through the conversion to ensure there is no gap in orders or communication. Both of these priorities will have an impact on the supplier.

- There is also no alignment for the supplier's initiative to review packaging. It's possible this might not be the best area of focus if it will not resonate with the customer. There could be other reasons for this priority such as cost or new trends in packaging technology, which are both valid reasons but they will not resonate with the customer. If the packaging review was not absolutely necessary, it would be advisable to allocate the resources to get through the system conversion and perhaps develop some items specifically to support a discount banner.

The first version of your priority alignment chart should not be the final outcome. It is important to assess what the relationship looks like with the customer and determine if priorities need to change. As we have discussed, with some minor changes, this supplier could be much more closely aligned to the customer. The planning process is the time to make these changes.

It's also very beneficial to create the core of your annual plan with the customer from this chart. Focus on the areas where there's alignment and either address areas where there's no alignment or avoid them if they do not have a negative long-term impact.

Working with retailers can be very challenging. Have a plan and do not expect everything to happen quickly. These are large organizations and your priorities are not high on their list.

The Romans implemented a system of milestones on the roads they built 2,000 years ago. Designed to help the traveller understand where they were on their journey, every milestone included the direction to Rome. This concept can be very effective in developing the relationship with your retail customers. You can develop your own milestones to understand where you are on the journey. Always remember which direction the retailer is heading, which is your Rome!

Your business priorities should be reviewed throughout the year for progress. If you've set your own milestones they should be the core of the update. The respective owners should report on progress and remember to include the impact on your customers. The customer should recognize the work being done and understand how this work supports their offering.

MAKING PROGRESS

One of the biggest challenges for suppliers selling to today's retailers is that it can be very difficult to see progress with the relationship. Category managers change frequently, stock price volatility has made it difficult to commit to long term strategic direction and people at different levels of organizations have different perspectives on initiatives. Just as a supplier feels like they are making progress the category manager will change or the focus will shift from cost control to sales.

One of the people I have a great deal of respect for was the president at one of our local dairies, a dairy farmer who had taken on the challenge of running the dairy. He would work long hours in his executive role, then go home to work two to three hours more on the farm.

One day an employee asked him why he did this. The hours at the dairy were long and could be very challenging, how could he drive home and spend hours on a tractor cutting hay? His response was that he could turn around and see what he had accomplished. He could see the rows of fresh mown hay from the seat of the tractor. His work at the dairy rarely provided this sense of accomplishment. It's true that working with today's retailers can be a grueling marathon and the finish line continues to move further out. It's not for the faint of heart!

Suppliers and retailers are all trying to sell food. With a better understanding of the priorities and challenges we each face, there could be a much more effective value chain. With a good understanding of your customer's priorities and a plan to deliver results you will develop a very prosperous relationship. This relationship will afford you the luxury of educating them about your business and the challenges you face. Together you can find a more productive relationship where you both accomplish your objectives.

As I said at the start, selling food products should be such a simple business. Do you see now how selling food products can be such a business? Understand the priorities of your customers, build a business model that delivers a profit, develop alignment with your customer's priorities, produce a product, deliver it to the retailer and watch the consumer put it in their shopping cart!

SAMPLE CHART FOR YOUR BUSINESS

CUSTOMER

RETAILER'S PRIORITIES

YOUR BUSINESS PRIORITIES

SAMPLE CHART FOR YOUR BUSINESS

CUSTOMER

RETAILER'S PRIORITIES

YOUR BUSINESS PRIORITIES

SAMPLE CHART FOR YOUR BUSINESS

CUSTOMER

RETAILER'S PRIORITIES

YOUR BUSINESS PRIORITIES

SAMPLE CHART FOR YOUR BUSINESS

CUSTOMER

RETAILER'S PRIORITIES

YOUR BUSINESS PRIORITIES

THE RECIPE FOR SUCCESS

Developing a productive working relationship with retailers is a complicated process. I have identified the 10 most important points that will get the items in the shopping cart.

1. Productive relationships require both parties to understand and respect each other. Ensure your organization understands and respects the priorities and challenges of retailers.
2. Educate retailers on your organization including the priorities and challenges you face. Do this succinctly and respect their knowledge of the industry.
3. Develop a unique strategy for each retailer.
4. Follow your item through the entire value chain to ensure it delivers the experience to consumers as you had intended.
5. Subscribe to the philosophy that products are sold when they go through the cash register at the store.
6. Food safety should always be top of mind.
7. Stay on top of trends. These opportunities deliver incremental sales, profit and position your items differently in the market.
8. Find opportunities where you can deliver value to retailers beyond sales and profit. You will benefit if you provide expertise and solutions.
9. Understand the competitive environment in which they operate. Let them do their job and remember you are one of many.
10. Respect the systems and processes that allow retailers to operate but never lose sight of how important relationships are to your business.

THE LANGUAGE OF RETAILERS

It is important to understand what your customers are saying and speak their language. Every industry has its own terms and abbreviations. I have listed some of the definitions for the language of retail.

Absolute sales: Total sales, regardless of physical or other changes.

Cherry picking: A term used by retailers to describe consumers who travel from one store to the other only buying the items on sale.

Comparable sales (comp sales): Sales in a location where there has been no major renovation or change to the product mix. Used by analysts as the truest measure of a retailer's performance from one comparable period in time to another.

Control label: The products available that the retailer develops and sells. These items usually get preferred shelf space because the retailer derives more profit. Synonymous with private label.

Cube: The amount of product that can go on a truck.

Direct Store Delivery (DSD): Some products do not go through the warehouse, they go directly to the store. These items are often guaranteed sale, which are merchandised by the supplier (commercial bread, soft drinks or dairy), short code date products or they have small sales and the vendor understands the item better than the retailer.

Display Ready Pallet (DRP): Product packed by a supplier on a pallet that can be positioned in the store and be ready for merchandising with minimal work from store staff. Often there is some POS with these. For example: Costco uses DRP's.

End cap: The shelving at the end of an aisle. Usually front ends (opposite the checkouts) will have fewer shelves and be designed to merchandise the higher volume ad items. The back ends (facing the rear of the store) will have more items and be used to merchandise lower volume ad items or themes.

Every Day Low Price (EDLP): A pricing philosophy that follows the premise consumers will support the store regularly where they will get the lowest overall shopping bill on the items they want to buy. There are no deep discount ads, just very good competitive pricing through out the store. Walmart follows the EDLP strategy.

Front end: The cash registers.

Grazing: A term used by retailers to describe consumers who eat product in the store before they pay (or not) for it.

Guaranteed sale: The supplier will reimburse the retailer for any product not sold at the best before date or after a specific holiday season. This is employed by retailers to protect against high shrink on items when they do not perform as expected.

Health and Beauty Aids (HABA): A department where over the counter (OTC) medication, shampoo, soap and other beauty care products are merchandised. Synonymous with Health and Beauty Care (HBC).

Health and Beauty Care (HBC): A department where OTC medication, shampoo, soap and other beauty care products are merchandised. Synonymous with Health And Beauty Aids (HABA).

High-Low: A pricing philosophy that follows the premise that consumers will be attracted by deep discounts on advertised items. Shelf pricing is higher on other items to support the investment in the ad items. Sobeys and Loblaws would follow a high-low strategy.

Home Meal Replacement (HMR): Department in a food store designed to offer items that are ready to eat. They can be merchandised hot for immediate consumption or cold for take home.

In line: Items merchandised in the regular aisle.

Merchandising: The business unit within the retailer responsible for determining which items will be listed, where they will be purchased, the retail price, where they will be displayed for sale, selecting flyer items and implementing theme promotions.

Off shelf: A secondary display of products away from their regular shelf position. Often these are end caps or floor displays.

Operations: The business unit within the retailer responsible for running the stores, managing all controllable expenses (such as labour) and implementing the plans developed by the merchandisers.

Plan-o-gram (POGs): The predetermined placement of items for a particular section of shelving. Retailers develop plan-o-grams to maximize sales and profit within a category. Other factors such as control label SKUs, preferred vendors and listing fees are considered when building POGs.

Private label: The products available that the retailer develops and sells. These items usually get preferred shelf space because the retailer derives more profit. Synonymous with control label.

Product Look Up (PLU): Codes embedded in the retailers systems to identify specific items that do not have UPC codes or bar codes for scanning, such as two bagels a customer has self selected in a bag and written on the code. Cashiers must input these as the item goes through the checkout. Often used for produce and bulk bakery items. The produce industry has standardized PLU codes which are used around the world. Some produce items now have PLU codes that will scan at the cash register.

Retail: The price point.

Sales per man hour/sales per labour hour: The total dollar sales divided by the number of labour hours used. This is a method of comparing results across departments and divisions.

Sales per square foot: Total sales divided by the retail square footage of a location. Sales per square foot usually exclude back room (warehouse) space.

Service level: The percentage of product actually delivered to the store relative to their order. Service level is calculated by dividing the actual number of cases delivered by the number of cases ordered.

Shelf pricing: The regular retail price of items in the store

Shrink: The value of goods the retailers purchase from suppliers that never make it through the cash register. Shrink is caused by damages, code date expiration, theft, product degradation or data integrity errors.

Short code date products: Products that have a short period of time before the best before date expires. These are more challenging for retailers as there is a limited time to get the item through the supply chain, into the store and into the shopping cart.

Stock Keeping Unit (SKU): The term used to describe an item or product.

Supply chain: The business unit within the retailer responsible for procuring, warehousing and distributing products.

Top line: Sales, which is THE priority for any business.

Universal Product Code (UPC): A 12 digit number and associated bar code on each unique product. These numbers are used to track the item through the retailers' systems.

Volume: Sales through the cash registers. Volume can be dollars or units.

Wing: A small unit beside the end cap. Some retailers use these to merchandise items that do not work well on regular shelving such as a display of birthday cake candles. Other retailers will change these to display higher margin complementary products to tie in to the large volume item on the end to draw the consumer in with the ad item, then sell them something profitable.

RESOURCES

CHAPTER 2

www.loblaw.ca

www.sobeys.com

www.empireco.ca

www.metro.ca

www.costco.ca

www.costco.com

www.walmart.ca

www.walmart.com

www.target.ca

www.target.com

www.wholefoodsmarket.com

CHAPTER 3

www.jimpattison.com/food/default.aspx

www.tnt-supermarket.com

www.gianttiger.com

www.coopatlantic.ca

www.calgarycoop.ca

www.coopconnection.ca

www.presidentschoice.ca

www.compliments.ca

www.metro.ca/home.en.html

CHAPTER 4

www.sobeyscorporate.com/en/video.aspx.

www.walmart.com/global-responsibility/
environment-sustainability/truck-fleet

www.cpma.ca

CHAPTER 5

www.mygfsi.com

www.brcglobalstandards.com.

www.canadagap.com.

www.onfarmfoodsafety.ca.

CHAPTER 6

www.phac-aspc.gc.ca/hp-ps/hl-mvs/oic-oac/

www.heartandstroke.ca

www.diabetes.ca

www.guidingstars.ca

www.presidentschoice.ca/en_CA/familypage/
PCBlueMenuPage.html

www.walmartcommunity.com/
hunger-nutrition/#view

www.sobeys.com/en/departments/
jamie-oliver

www.inspection.gc.ca
CFIA

CHAPTER 7

www.statcan.gc.ca

www.vinelandresearch.com

CHAPTER 8

www.statcan.gc.ca

www.cedarbaygrilling.com

CHAPTER 9

www.loblaw.ca

www.sobeys.com

www.empireco.ca

www.metro.ca

www.costco.ca

www.costco.com

www.walmart.ca

www.walmart.com

www.target.ca

www.target.com

www.wholefoodsmarket.com

ACKNOWLEDGEMENTS

This proved to be a much tougher project that I anticipated it to be... writing a book is so much more than content on a page.

The encouragement and support from Jennifer and the rest of our family has been the best it could be. Her understanding of the roller coaster ride of self employment has made it possible. My mother shaped my values and my father has been an invaluable resource as I ventured out on my own.

My colleagues in the food industry have taught me so much. When you leave a position at a food retailer you know who your friends are. They call you back because you are you, not because you can influence their career or get their item in an ad.

My clients made this complete. Without insight in to your businesses and the challenges you face, I could not have brought the full perspective.

Friends and mentors in the speaking industry said you have to do a book, they were right.

Darrell Munro, George Condon and Cynthia Martin pushed me to get it right. You helped me turn a word document in to an attractive, accurate and articulate piece of work that I am proud to share.

ABOUT THE AUTHOR

Peter Chapman understands the Canadian food industry. His career started in a small grocery store in Fredericton N.B. where he was told on the first day "we treat our customers right here, if you don't, you will have to find another job." This was the start of a career in marketing; understanding and anticipating the needs of customers.

After finishing school, Peter took a summer job with Atlantic Wholesalers, Loblaw's Atlantic regional office at the time. This was the beginning of a 19-year career with Canada's largest food retailer. He held positions in various departments, including merchandising, marketing, advertising and real estate.

With Loblaw's decision in 2007 to consolidate merchandising functions in Ontario, Peter decided it was time to start a new chapter in his career. Peter's company, GPS Business Solutions, provides services to producers and manufacturers who want to increase their sales to large, centrally structured retailers or specialty food stores. Peter also speaks to audiences of producers, processors and industry associations to help them understand food retailing.

An in-depth knowledge of the retail landscape and the Canadian consumer are invaluable to producers and manufacturers who want to grow their sales. Peter has considerable experience – from developing relationships with suppliers throughout the supply chain, to retail merchandising.

He is passionate about helping you understand the retailers and get your items in to the shopping cart of the consumer more often.

Peter and his family live in Bedford, Nova Scotia.